COUPLE
CONVERSATION

DISCARD

COUPLE
CONVERSATION

THEODORE CHAFFEE

the art of
creating intimacy

BEACON HILL PRESS
OF KANSAS CITY

ISBN: 978-0-8341-2374-8

Printed in the
United States of America

Cover Design: Arthur Cherry
Internal Design: Sharon Page

Library of Congress Cataloging-in-Publication Data
Chaffee, Theodore E., 1951-
    Couple conversation : the art of creating intimacy / Theodore E. Chaffee.
       p. cm.
    ISBN-13: 978-0-8341-2374-8 (pbk.)
    ISBN-10: 0-8341-2374-6 (pbk.)
    1. Intimacy (Psychology)—Religious aspects—Christianity. 2. Conversation—Reli-
gious aspects—Christianity. 3. Marriage—Religious aspects—Christianity. I. Title.
    BV4597.53.I55C43 2008
    248.8'44—dc22

                                                                    2008014292

10 9 8 7 6 5 4 3 2 1

CONTENTS

Our task in this technological era is not to invent a new theory of communication or a new theory of therapy, but to develop the art and craft of intimate expression.

—Thomas Moore

Reality has been understood through much of recorded history as an integrated and mutually interacting web of body, mind, soul, and spirit. When we face problems in our human reality, we can often understand those problems as dysfunctions in the way these different levels of reality interacted with each other.

—Michael Lerner

Love the Lord your God with all your heart and with all your soul and with all your mind and with all your strength.

—Mark 12:30

INTRODUCTION
RISING HIGH AND
SEARCHING DEEP

୶

So here you are, you and your partner, trying to blend two distinct lives using conversation as a type of adhesive to glue together the joys, sorrows, pressures, and changes that come flying at you every day. You try to connect. You try to build some kind of intimate continuity. But it's not working all that well. Half the time the stuff of life flies by you so fast you hardly have time to talk about it. Then when you do sit down to talk, the conversational glue just doesn't seem to stick.

You would like to radio for help. "Houston, we have a problem. We're in the same room, speaking the same language, struggling for the same outcome, but we may as well be on different planets."

You're not alone. This feeling is very common among couples. The problem is not that you're on different planets but that you're in different dimensions.

And while it may feel as if those dimensions are part of *The Twilight Zone,* they're actually very familiar aspects of your everyday experiences. You can easily identify those aspects, or dimensions, as your body, mind, soul, and spirit. The problem is, each dimension speaks a language all its own. When these languages get babbled in your conversation, your sense of connection with each other evaporates like sweat on a ghost.

Bob and Jessica understand how this happens. Their experience may sound familiar to you.

Jessica grew up the second of three sisters. "We were very close." Her eyes seem to cull memories from the crease between the wall and ceiling as she talks. "Maybe too close. I mean, we shared everything. We always seemed to know what each other was feeling." Her eyes flash an abrupt return to earth as she interrupts herself. "We had our spats—believe me. And when we were fighting, well, you just wouldn't want to be around for that." Her smile breaks into laughter.

"My dad couldn't stand it. He always found some reason to leave the house or putter around downstairs until the coast was clear. But when we went through tough times, we would sit up for hours talking things through. We would laugh, we would cry, we would hug, hash things out; we would just share what was going on.

"I guess I just expected Bob and I would be like that too—just sharing our life, our thoughts, our feelings. But whenever I try to talk with him about what's going on for me inside, he turns official and instructive. He doesn't seem to understand what I need at those times."

From Jessica's standpoint, these expectations seem legit. She's comfortable with a fairly deep level of communication and wants to experience that with her husband. But Bob doesn't get it. He's not a villain or a terrible communicator—he's trying to help. He views emotion as many in our culture are taught: feelings are for the most part inconvenient and need to be resolved and forgotten as soon as possible. "I figure that whatever is bothering her, let's get to the bottom of it, get it resolved, and move on."

Bob's responses to Jessica feel stone-cold. He's trying to help her find the cause of her unpleasant feelings and remove it. But because he operates from an intellectual, problem-solving point of view, his response doesn't match with Jessica's emotion. Bob

One of the teachers of the law came and heard them debating. Noticing that Jesus had given them a good answer, he asked him, "Of all the commandments, which is the most important?"

"The most important one" answered Jesus, "is this: 'Hear, O Israel, the Lord our God, the Lord is one. Love the Lord your God with all your heart and with all your soul and with all your mind and with all your strength."

—Mark 12:28-30

Sex and the Simple Book

Sex and intimacy are often confused. Sometimes couples use the words interchangeably, as in "We were intimate last night." Actually, each of your four dimensions has its own healthy and vibrant expressions of sexuality, but to explore all those enticing possibilities is beyond the scope of this simple book. While I hope that your love life will improve as you work through these chapters, we'll be focusing primarily on the conversational foundations of intimacy rather than its sexual expressions.

is trapped in the dimension of mind while Jessica is speaking from her soul.

This frustrates Bob as well. "When these conversations come to an end, she says I didn't hear her or care about her feelings. But I did hear her, and I do care. I get frustrated that she doesn't listen to my advice. She wants me to understand her feelings, but she doesn't want to hear what I have to say."

Sound familiar? The more Bob talks, the more lost he becomes. It's as though he's trying hard to explain the laws of buoyancy while Jessica just wants to take a swim. No matter how desperately and sincerely he tries, no matter how astute his observations and insights, no matter how far he drives along this analytical road, he'll never reach her. She's in another dimension, one she desperately wants him to join her in.

Crisscrossing the rational and emotional dimensions is just one of several ways to babble a conversation. Whenever you speak from one dimension, you use a certain, well-defined way of talking. If your spouse listens and responds to you in that same dimension, bingo—the connection is made. When you and your partner operate in different dimensions, crisscrossing your meanings and intentions, you'll likely feel more distant than when you started talking. Does crisscrossing ever happen with you and your partner? Do you ever babble?

FROM MUCK TO REMARKABLE

Why is this all so difficult? It almost sounds like a paradox: two souls joined in love, admiration, and trust, living a life of commitment to each other—yet finding it almost impossibly hard to talk. What's so difficult about talking? Try answering that question, and you find that the questions multiply.

Why do we often not talk when we really need to?

Why does it always come down to one of us (usually me) insisting that we talk?

Why do we sometimes completely misunderstand each other?

Why do I sometimes feel after talking that we're farther apart than before?

Though the answers to these questions can be elusive, failure to find them can devastate your relationship. Failed conversation allows life's tensions to run amuck. To one degree or another, we all know the frustration of facing life together without that fluid, creative, and connective conversation. The stresses and strains of normal life place great demands on intimate connection, bogging down the flow of energy, stifling the zest of passion, creating troubled waters on the sea of love.

At times it can even make you question your love. We've all been knocked off an emotional mountaintop as our conversation spirals downward, deflating our best efforts and making a mockery of our preconceived notions of relationship. No one wants to live there. Wouldn't it be better to return to those happy, innocent days at the beginning of your relationship?

It may seem so, but that's neither the issue nor a possibility. The challenge before you today lies not so much in rekindling that long-faded spark of burning attraction and first love but in creating and maintaining a lasting flame of connection, depth, trust, and beauty.

Are we dreaming the impossible dream? To talk together in such a way, suggesting that the tensions of life and relationship morph into solved problems, lived dreams, and realized intimacy seems idealistic at best. Hocus-pocus! We would all love it, but who can perform such miracles? Can you? Can you really enjoy conversation that separates the wheat from the chaff, the remarkable from the mundane, and spurs you on in your search for the fullness of life and the wonder of intimacy?

Why not? Turning the muck to the remarkable is what couple conversation is all about. That's why it's called an art.

It may be difficult. It will require effort. And when done right, it becomes a unique, creative, and lasting thing of beauty.

Of course, it's unrealistic to expect every conversation to carry wonder in its backpack. But to those who are aware of its presence, to those who learn to expect the miracle, couple conversation will reveal itself time and time again to enrich, strengthen, deepen, and dignify your relationship from top to bottom.

If you're reading through these pages, it's your desire to build a bridge over the troubled waters of your relationship; things have gotten mucky over time, and you're ready to roll up your sleeves and get to work. This book aims to show you how.

THE FOUR DIMENSIONS OF INTIMACY

Intimate conversation begins with two simple questions:

Who am I?

Who are you?

These questions could be answered in a number of interesting ways, but in this book we'll focus on four aspects or dimensions of your personality and growth.

Like a majestic Bach chorale, you're composed in four-part harmony. You have your physical part, your body; your thinking part, your mind; your inward, psychological part, your soul; and your outward, social part, your spirit. Scientists of human development use these four dimensions to track the progress of an individual over the lifespan. Jesus used these four dimensions to explain how we should totally love God. You may want to pause for a moment or two and ponder these aspects of your life. Seen in this way, you really are a very interesting and complex person. It's no wonder the one you love loves you.

But you hit a snag when your spouse asks you who you are. You're bound to answer with a question or two of your own:

Who am I right now?

Who was I 10 years ago?

Who Are You?

Talk with your partner about which you each most resemble intellectually—

A sponge: just soaking everything up

A steel trap: locking onto a few important facts

A popcorn popper: always bursting with thoughts and ideas

A tortoise: you take your time, but you're always sure you're right

Who was I 10 months ago?

Even 10 minutes ago?

These four dimensions in you are organic and restless: they constantly move, shift, and grow. Your body doesn't look or act the way it did five years ago. You also think differently, dream differently, and believe differently than you used to.

Some of these changes may be due to outside events and influences in your life, like a move, a miscarriage, or meeting someone new and exciting. Other changes may seem to develop from deep within you regardless of what's happening around you, like simple maturity, an illness, or a blossoming passion for faith or nature. Either way, you've changed, and you continue to change. Even now, reading this book, you're becoming somewhat different than the person your partner slept with last night.

The same holds true, of course, for your husband or wife. Patterns of shifting, developing, and changing are at work in both of you. The agony and the ecstasy of intimacy are locked together in the fact that each of you changes in your own sweet way and in your own sweet time. No amount of soul-searching, book-reading, or answer-questing will ever lead you to a full understanding of that process. But intimacy consists primarily of a continual, multidimensional invitation to love and mutual support through a life riddled with pleasure and pain, surprises and drudgery, comedy and tragedy, challenge and disappointment.

The key to mixing life and love to create intimacy lies in how you talk about it. Change without conversation creates distance. And, despite what you think, conversation that weaves your lives together, though sometimes difficult, lies well within you ability. As your conversation becomes less confusing and more engaging, varied, and enriched, it will evolve from a drab and fruitless communication to a living art.

CLIMBING THE OLD APPLE TREE

Intimacy grows from the ground up, like an old apple tree. And our climb in learning intimate conversation will follow the same natural pattern.

You'll start with the basic roots of conversation: good listening. Section one introduces the foundational skills of listening, the responsibilities of the listener, and practical ways to make your listening better.

The deep roots of listening lead to the connective conversation necessary for the smooth running of your practical, daily concerns. In this style of conversation, symbolized by the tree trunk, you'll explore the physicality of your life together: your tasks, your work, your chores, your fun, your schedules. You'll consider the boundaries that both define and protect your relationship. This style of conversation, called light talk, corresponds to the body.

You'll then move on to the mind. When presented with a problem, you may have said to each other, "Let's put our heads together on this one." In that case you use your minds to think, reason, and figure things out. This style of conversation is called mind talk, symbolized by the branches of the apple tree. Mind talk involves the analytical, reasoning aspects of your relationship, but I must advise caution here! As we'll see in section three, not every mind makes sense in the same way.

You'll turn next to your soul. As the leaf mysteriously takes the light of the sun and creates nourishment for the entire tree, so your soul reaches out to the intangibles of life like beauty, feeling, and memory and creates stability and permanence in your inner being. When you share these inner realities with each other, you use soul talk. Being intimate on this level creates what many refer to as being soul mates. Most couples desire this closeness, and in section four you'll learn how to make it happen consistently.

The Game of Life

A basketball player masters five skills: running, dribbling, passing, shooting, and jumping. A dedicated player may spend hours focused on improving in just one of these areas. But in the game the five skills flow together in a beautiful and graceful flow of athletic movement.

The same is true in conversation. You'll focus on gaining skills in each one of five areas: listening, light talk, mind talk, soul talk, and heart talk. These will be treated separately as you improve. But in real life, your conversation will beautifully and gracefully flow through all dimensions to create a firm, long-lasting intimacy.

The fourth style of conversation, represented by the apple itself, is called heart talk. Heart talk has to do with the ways in which you take the thoughts and feelings inside of you and move them outward into the world. Heart talk changes things. The urge within you that pushes this forward carries many names, including your will, your spirit, and your intention. Have either of you been called strong-willed? Does the word "stubborn" ever come up in your home? Though heart talk has many broad applications in your life and your spirituality, in your relationship it begins with one simple question: How do you and your partner influence each other?

GETTING STARTED

While in the following pages you'll learn to build intimacy in all four dimensions, it's unlikely that you'll need an equal amount of work in each of them. Your relationship has aspects that are very strong, aspects that others observe and possibly envy. You also have areas that need some work. Your patterns of connection may have, for good reasons, developed well in some areas and not in others. It's that way with all relationships.

The chart on page 20 provides a quick reference to help identify your areas of strength and those areas that need work. As a general rule, like healthy trees, healthy couples develop themselves in all four areas.

As you begin your work together, you may be tempted to go directly to your most underdeveloped area. Before you do, consider doing the following. First, be sure to read and practice the listening skills described in the first chapter. All the chapters on talking are built on good listening. The health of every tree depends on the health of its roots.

Second, take time to enjoy and celebrate your strengths. Don't completely skip chapters simply because you're already good at the skills they discuss. When you look only at what hasn't been working, improvement can be a long, difficult process. Take full advantage of your strengths to build confidence, create joy, and demonstrate the wonder and workings of your unique relationship.

You won't find a mechanical, cookie-cutter approach to communication in this book. Conversation, as the subtitle suggests, is an art, not a science. You won't be asked to squeeze yourselves into a mold that someone else has said should fit you. As you work through this book together, grow your own intimate patterns, and develop them in ways that feel good to you. No other couple clicks exactly the way you do.

Styles of Conversation

	Deep Listening	Light Talk	Mind Talk	Soul Talk	Heart Talk
You're building intimacy if . . .	• You feel attended to • Eye contact is satisfactory • You report similar understandings of the same conversation • After talking, you have a pretty good idea of what your partner thinks about a subject	• You feel connected even when apart • You have a basic knowledge of the other's day (appointments, tasks, etc.) • You can talk for hours • Your daily life is somewhat organized	• You can debate without putdowns • You both think the other one is smart • You make a good team • Joint tasks work well • Offering your viewpoint is fun	• You're able to express your feelings • You've talked about the future • Beliefs and convictions are shared and respected • You and your partner really know each other	• You both have an equal say • You always feel respected • Compliments are given and received freely • Differences are worked through with minimal conflict • You don't feel manipulated
Your intimacy needs work if . . .	• You spend little time talking • Interruptions occur • Little or no eye contact is made • Volume increases often occur • Attention-getting ploys are frequent • Each has a different understanding of the same conversation	• You're unaware of the other's daily tasks • Very little time is taken to coordinate schedules • Family events are unknown to you • You feel that you live parallel lives	• One is seen as less rational than the other • Debates become lectures • Decisions are not mutual • Decisions just don't make sense	• Feelings are not shared • What's inside is not talked about • You sometimes seem like a mystery to each other • There are parts of life history that are not talked about • There's a dark side that's never mentioned	• One clams up and lets the other decide • Differences lead to unresolved conflict • You're unsure of what your partner wants • Insults or name-calling happen • Threats or violence of any kind occur

section one
DEEP LISTENING

The first duty of love is to listen.
—Paul Tillich

*All of a man's life among his kind is nothing other
than a battle to seize the ear of others.*
—Milan Kundera

one

THE LISTENING EAR

∿

It began humbly enough. Perhaps in a few stolen minutes before class or, like Avery and Michelle, in a café after a busy day. Do you remember the first time you realized your spouse was really listening to you? Like a seed in the ground, that moment may have passed unnoticed by anyone. But not by you! You felt it. You knew it.

Avery and Michelle met while standing in line at a local coffee shop; she ordered chai tea, and he ordered café Americano. Unfortunately, the barista mistakenly switched cups, and the two collectively sipped and sputtered in dismay over their drinks. The barista apologized quickly and served up their correct beverages. While they waited, Avery introduced himself, and Michelle self-consciously fiddled with her necklace. She loved his outgoing personality, and he felt drawn to her quiet sweetness.

They decided to meet the following morning to see if the barista could get it right. A month later, they were still meeting for coffee and an occasional dinner date. Two months later, Avery proposed. Michelle planned a June wedding, and Avery surprised her with a cruise.

And they lived happily ever after—or at least until a series of misunderstandings led to what they now call their honeymoon disaster. But more about that later.

All love, yours as well as Avery and Michelle's, begins its life as a tiny seed forming roots. A tough little strand breaks through the shell of its seed and sends its fingers down into the soil, seeking the nutrients that will sustain growth and health throughout its life. For roots, as for lovers, this search never ends. It keeps growing deeper and wider in pursuit of its goal. Using tiny, delicate tips called root hairs, roots absorb the necessary elements from the soil and move them up to the rest of the tree. The trunk, branches, and leaves all depend on this nourishment for life, growth, and beauty. A tree can be only as healthy as its roots.

A loving listener follows this pattern by probing and digging deep into the heart and soul of the other to find nourishment for the relationship. Deep listening anchors strong conversation, and strong conversation, in turn, helps produce a vibrant, healthy intimacy.

BULKING UP

Every conversation needs two people: a talker and a listener. This seems pretty simple, but it's amazing how often we forget it. It's so easy to talk! And sometimes we even think our talking accomplishes something. So on we go—talk, talk, jabber, jabber, gab, jabber, gab, gab, talk. It happens every day. But nothing is added to your relationship until someone listens. You may as well be that poor tree falling in the forest, wasting all those crackling and sizzling airborne vibrations when no one is there to hear.

On the other hand, when listening happens, those sizzling airborne vibrations of your voice actually produce something. What you say instantly becomes part of your shared experience,

The Listening Day

Once a month declare a "Special Listening Day." During this day, dedicate yourself to listening to your partner all day long. Rather than expect the gift of listening to be returned, stay in the listening mode. Keep engaging. Keep asking. Keep showering your attention with love and gusto. Take time at the end of the day to reflect on what you've heard and learned.

This is also a great trick to try on your kids. You may be amazed at what you hear from them, but probably not as amazed as they'll be that you listened to them so intently.

part of your relationship. It may be a small part, as when you ask for a small favor or comment on the attitude of the cashier at the grocery store. At other times conversation adds in large chunks, as when you talk about your mother or relate a frightening experience.

Listening closes the circle. When your voice finds a listening ear, it happens. The giver finds the receiver. From that moment on, whatever you're saying enters the realm of togetherness. Some is forgotten quite quickly—no need to deny that. But remembered or forgotten at some level, what you've said and how you've said it lies there between you. Whether in small bites or large chunks, this beautiful exchange of talking and listening continually adds bulk to your relationship. This bulk settles in deeply, providing stability, like ballast on a sailboat or feet on an adolescent boy. It keeps upright what seems very shaky.

In this way your relationship resembles the miracle of the standing tree. And what a miracle it is! It may be 70 or 80 feet tall. It opens its leaves like tiny sails to the breezes and sways in the wind. As tall and as comparatively slender as it is, however, under normal conditions it remains upright. You walk without worry under these magnificent living structures in the forest or along the street. The thought of one falling scarcely enters your mind.

What keeps these tall, heavy objects from tipping over? The tree's foothold stretches both deep and wide. The extensive structure of roots under the ground forms an immense, clinging network that firmly grasps the earth and won't let go. As long as that grasp remains healthy, the tree will stand to face nearly all combinations of wind and weather. Separate a tree from its roots, however, as lumberjacks do every day, and it inevitably falls. Roots provide stability.

In a similar fashion, the process of good listening brings a sense of stability and constancy to your relationship. As you pay concentrated attention to what you hear, as you open the doors for an ever-deepening conversation, as you provide a listening ear to the expression of thoughts, feelings, or memories that have lain long-hidden deep within, you anchor your relationship deeply in the soil of your soul.

FEEDING LOVE

In addition to stability, your relationship also needs a constant flow of nourishment. Good love needs good food. Malnutrition poses a serious threat to your relationship's health. A lack of listening paves the path to that arid state. A couple who stops listening stops sharing, stops thinking, stops planning, stops laughing. By listening to each other, you release a fountain of new information, new perspectives, new ideas, new plans, and new jokes.

The constant flow of newness jolts your relationship with life and interest. Bored? Who has time to be bored? Boredom is a stranger in a listening relationship. Some couples confuse themselves by inverting the connection between listening and boredom. Have you ever heard this statement?—"I'm bored with you, so I've just stopped listening." Actually it works the other way around: "I've stopped listening to you, so I'm bored."

After 14 years of marriage to Jessica, Bob shared how their listening habits had changed. "I was in the Navy when we were dating and during those first few years of our marriage. There were times when I was deployed, and we wouldn't see each other for weeks. When I returned we would just gobble up every second we could to be together. I remember longing to hear her voice. It didn't matter what she was talking about—I just wanted to listen. I soaked in every word. Somehow it relaxed me, made me feel good, filled me up after all those weeks on the ship.

"Now it's different—I'll admit it. I don't listen the way I used to. I'll let her rattle on, but I have one ear tuned to the TV or one eye on the paper. I guess I can't blame her for feeling alone."

Jessica chimes in. "We've tried things to spice up our marriage: a vacation together, some new friends, theater tickets, stuff like that. And we've had some fun—we know how to have fun together when we want to. But soon we drag back down into that old routine—as if there's something missing."

Jessica has touched on a strategy many couples employ when boredom creeps in. You may have tried a few of them yourself: buy a new car, get a different job, experiment with new sexual experiences, have another baby, or take an exotic vacation. All of these have their place as solutions to various problems, but all solutions fail to solve the boredom problem unless they're accompanied by a new commitment to listen to each other. As Bob said, there's a fullness and sense of pleasure that comes with good listening. Listening remains the most extensive and least expensive path to a thriving, well-fed relationship.

The strength of your relationship is not found in how often you talk but in how deeply you listen to each other. Imagine yourself tunneling deeply and widely into the mind and heart of the one you love. The more you find there, the stronger your love can be. The more deeply you listen, the higher you grow. The farther down into the soul you dig, the stronger your relationship will be in the face of the winds and storms of life. To secure intimacy, follow the roots of listening.

two

THE ROOT OF
LISTENING 1
RELAX AND OBSERVE

There must be 50 ways to listen badly. Bad listening skills grow like weeds during childhood and adolescence, because parents, teachers, principals, and various self-appointed advisors who lecture endlessly provide the perfect backdrop for kids to hone these skills to an exact and elegant science.

Double-dipping is one commonly used strategy. This involves making minimal eye contact and faking enough attention to convince the talker that you're listening while you skillfully glance away at something that really interests you more. This strategy has a sub-strategy that uses ears instead of eyes to divert your attention elsewhere. Using distractions of the eye or ear help relieve the tension of the conversation.

Another well-used strategy might be called the false focus, in which the listener uses focused facial expression to indicate rapt attention. Intense eye contact, arched eyebrows, and the occasional "hmmm" of affirmation merely disguise the fact that inside your head you're a million miles away. Pretending to be

Conversational Pet Peeves

Think about the two or three things your partner says or does during a conversation that really drive you crazy. You can hardly keep listening when these conversational pet peeves appear. When was the last time one of these pet peeves appeared? How did you handle it?

Can you think of any better ways you could handle it in the future?

present, the bad listener is really making vacation plans or day-dreaming of a beach far away or studying the details of the talker's face from forehead creases to nostril hairs with nothing less than scientific intensity.

A third, rather dangerous, strategy is called the crouching cat. In this case, the listener resembles a cat ready to pounce on the unsuspecting mouse. With mental muscles coiled like springs on a pogo stick, the crouching cat waits patiently for a brief break or hesitation in the talker. Even a small breath gives the listener time to pounce, blurting out in a long and steady flow all that you've been thinking about instead of actually listening.

Helpful as those skills may be in some situations, building intimacy is one project in which they definitely work against you. Intimacy requires good listening above all else. Holding on to these bad habits can end an intimate conversation as abruptly and unceremoniously as those long-handled canes that whisk a bad vaudeville performer off stage.

The good news is that just as you learned those richly nuanced bad habits, you can also easily learn and practice the skills required for intimate expression. Essentially there are only four, and the simplest way to remember them is to think of the acronym ROOT: Relax, Observe, Open Up, and Touch. Later on you'll see that each style of conversation has unique qualities, characteristics, and demands of the listener. All the listening tasks in this book, however, grow naturally and securely from these four skills.

RELAX

Like brain surgery and rock-climbing, good listening requires a cool, steady hand. While a certain flow of adrenaline or emotion keeps you at your best, an overflow can be disastrous. There are times when talking with your partner tests your cool.

Pushed through a hurricane of thoughts, desires, and intentions, you try hard to listen well. But the pressure inside you gradually builds until you find yourself overwhelmed by your responses.

In such circumstances, which happen nearly every day for many couples, you need to relax. You need to temper your own feelings, impulses, reactions, and opinions in order to better focus on your partner. Developing skills in self-regulation is among the most significant of a good listener's tasks. You want to stay in the position of listener as long as possible. You don't want to interrupt or steal the focus of the conversation from your partner. To stay focused on your partner you'll need to sooth yourself.

Relax.

Rest.

Soothe.

Chill.

Get a grip.

All of this is much easier said than done.

How do you control yourself when your emotions are pushing you over a conversational cliff? People develop their own methods of staying calm on the edge. Some use deep breathing. Some count to 10 silently. Holding a physical object such as a small stone or a significant piece of jewelry can also help.

But what happens when these personal strategies don't work? What happens when you just can't relax? "Flooding" is a term often used to describe this feeling of being overwhelmed, over-stimulated, or over the edge. It feels as if you can't bear to hear another word without bursting. When this happens, don't try to fake it. Don't pretend you're cool, calm, and collected when actually inside you're ready to explode. Instead, call time out.

"Time out" simply means "Stop the conversation right now, and give me some time to breathe." When it comes to conver-

You can observe a lot just by watching.
—Attributed to Yogi Berra

Need a Break?

When was the last time you needed a time out—not when you were naughty and needed to sit in the corner but when you started to elevate emotionally during a conversation until you just couldn't talk or listen anymore?

How does your partner feel when you reach that point?

sation, healthy couples know as much about how and when to stop talking as they do about clarity, vocabulary, and empathic listening.

Devon and Maria, another young couple trying to establish good patterns in their marriage, often burn through this line of control like a flame in the autumn grass. Sometimes their disagreements turn ugly, even to the point of literally screaming at each other. Devon calls Maria vile names that you might expect to hear from a seasoned sailor while Maria proves her mettle by matching him name for name. She can even sometimes invent a few zingers of her own.

Following these outbursts, which can last for hours, each slumps back into a ball of pain, regret, remorse, and mistrust. The name-calling hurts deeply. Both Maria and Devon grew up in families marred by this continuous verbal abuse. They know how it can hurt, but they have no idea how to stop it. What can be done about these boundary-bashing conversations? The path to correction is difficult but clear.

With some guidance, Devon and Maria begin to think of their conversations as waves. The crest of the wave represents the most vicious and angry part of their communication. They imagine a typical conversation moving upward along the face of that wave. As they move upward, they get more and more upset and more and more angry. At what point do they lose it? At what point do they stop talking and start attacking each other?

Devon and Maria work hard to locate that line. They call it their "line of fire." All the wild and indiscriminate talking that happens above that line serves only to destroy their love and break their confidence in each other. This kind of talk has no place in their relationship.

Once they've identified this line of fire, they work backwards, gradually learning to stop the escalation before the urge to fight overwhelms them and sends them into a tizzy of destruction. First they watch for the physical signs leading up to that line: increased voice tension or volume, nervous fidgeting with the hands, increased flushing around the neck or face. Then they factor in other contributing factors, such as general mood, hot topics, and fatigue. This helps them become more aware of when blowouts are likely to occur and enables them to call a time out before things get out of hand.

If you and your spouse don't have an agreement about time outs, stop right now and make one. You may think that time outs, like certain breakfast cereals, are just for kids. But adults need them too. We never outgrow our need for a well-advised time out. It's vitally important that this step of relaxation be available to both of you at all times.

Here's how to set it up. First, prepare a signal. Either one of you may call time out at any time during any conversation by using this predetermined signal or phrase. Sometimes you'll be able to nicely explain why you want a time out, but often you may want to resort to a mutually understood signal and forget about further explanations. You both need to know that if the conversation is escalating beyond control, you have a quick and effective way to call a brief halt to talking to allow yourselves time to cool down.

Second, call time out courteously. This is not a time for dramatics or a mysterious silence. Use words that let your partner know that you care even if you can't listen right now.

Third, stop talking right now. Drop your gloves! Don't use the seconds immediately following a time-out call to get in a last shot at your spouse. One of our most barbaric sports, boxing, provides a lesson in this. Two combatants try with incredible intensity and diligence to bash each other's heads in for exactly two minutes at a time. When the bell rings to signal the end of the round, each one, regardless of emotional state and adrenaline flow, immediately drops the gloves and goes to a designated corner of the ring in silence.

Fourth, resume the conversation as soon as possible. A time

out must not be used as a way to escape a difficult topic. The reason for calling time out is to calm down, not to run away. The time needed for cooling may vary from couple to couple and from topic to topic, but the agreement always stays the same: we'll return to this conversation as soon as we can. It's a good idea for the one calling the time out to suggest a time to try again. This assures the other that you intend to resume.

Fifth, accept time out as a gift. Calling time out is not a condemnation. Whoever calls a time out does so for the sake of the relationship. Cling to that assumption. Think the very best of your loved one.

Relaxation, then, represents the first principle of good listening.

OBSERVE

"Honeymoon disaster"? Those are two words you never want to see locked together. But it is just that title that Avery and Michelle give to their newlywed drama. It turned out to be more a close call than an actual disaster, but it was close enough to brand Avery with a permanent understanding of the difference between seeing and observing.

We left Avery and Michelle happily sailing off on their honeymoon cruise, but things did not work out for them the way they had dreamed. Avery quickly took over their daily schedule. He eagerly filled their days with off-shore excursions, onboard pottery classes, and late-night dinner reservations; it was a once-in-a-lifetime experience, and he wanted to make the most of it for his new bride. Unfortunately, Michelle didn't share Avery's enthusiasm. She was thinking about more down time, more relaxing, more being alone with Avery. In short, she wanted less structure and more romance. During the hikes, Michelle was silent; Avery couldn't even coax a smile out of her on the dance floor.

Avery assumed that Michelle's withdrawal must relate to the

activities he had selected. So he redoubled his efforts in scheduling, nearly exhausting the long list of options provided by the cruise and wearing them both down to a frazzle. Frustrated at seeing his best efforts continue to go unrewarded, Avery finally reached his limit when Michelle excused herself from dinner one night and never returned. He found her quietly reading a magazine on deck. Avery couldn't keep the anger from his voice. "What is going on with you? Aren't you having fun? Talk to me. Let's work it out."

"I'm fine," she answered quietly.

But with each passing day, Michelle became more pensive. And Avery wondered, *What have I gotten myself into? This woman is ungrateful and moody. Nothing pleases her—she won't even talk to me!*

It seemed to Avery and Michelle that the honeymoon was over halfway through the cruise.

What's going on with this couple? It may look like a communication breakdown, but in fact Avery and Michelle are communicating very clearly. They just aren't using words. Avery is trying to say, "I love you," by planning activities together, and Michelle's tight-lipped "I'm fine" lets us know that whatever she wants to say, she's not using words to express it. They're flirting with disaster, because they're listening with their ears alone and not also with their eyes.

In deep listening the eye rivals the ear in importance. A good listener notices even the slightest signal. Think of how new parents observe every sound and motion of their infant. If their little girl rolls over in the night, they listen and watch. If their infant son puckers and drools, they contemplate the meaning of his actions. Every little gesture, every little sound, every little facial distortion evokes the highest level of attention.

Deep listeners, while perhaps not as flushed and excited as the new parent, observe with a similar dedication to detail. Understanding your partner involves more than merely hearing

Baseline Observations

Begin to compile, either in your mind or on paper, a list of your partner's facial expressions. Which are the most commonly seen varieties? What moods are often associated with each one? Which ones are rare but beautiful? Which ones signal trouble is on the way?

Compile a similar list focusing on your partner's movements or gestures and another listening to your partner's various tones of voice.

and deciphering the words that are said. In fact, words in their dictionary meaning only scratch the surface of conversation for the true listener. There's so much more to take in.

Think again of Avery and Michelle struggling along on their honeymoon cruise. How much did Avery miss by not observing carefully what Michelle was doing?

He didn't notice her sighs.

He failed to see her slight hesitation before joining in an activity.

He quickly backed away from her sudden, unexplained tearfulness.

He excused her shopping alone and returning late, "forgetting" they had something planned.

He ignored her new habit of looking off into space.

He totally missed the slight narrowing of her left eye when he mentioned the plans for tonight.

Avery really missed a boatload of messages here. Some were subtle, but others were pretty bold. Had he been a little more observant, his honeymoon would have contained a much better collection of memories. Here are some suggestions he wishes he had followed.

First, consider the sound of your partner's voice. The slightest deviations in vocal tone or intensity carry significance. Stress will show in a whisper of strain in the voice. Levels of volume or intensity speak of currents under the surface that struggle to be heard. Alert to these slight variations, you can catch on to what might be going on inside your spouse and open the conversation to greater understandings between the two of you.

Second, look for changes in your partner's body. What gestures, posture, position, and facial expressions are you seeing? These nonverbal messages provide clues to meaning. They point to the thoughts, feelings, or intentions behind the words you hear. Generally, the body holds the key to the interpretation of words.

This does not imply that nonverbal signals are a clear or consistent key. Your partner will use a wide variety of gestures and facial expressions. Observation will help you identify the patterns of use and will thus aid you in interpreting them. But in the end, understanding is an adventure. A wink means one thing at one time, something else at another. A smile may carry a host of clues: surprise, empathy, joy, satisfaction, and nervousness, to name just a few. Putting the clues together to make sense of what is said: this is the task of the observant listener.

Observation can help you in a number of ways. Did you notice that watching carefully plays a far different role in Avery and Michelle's honeymoon incident than it does with Maria and Devon's fights? For Avery, observing well would have opened up the conversation. Carefully noting the details of Michelle's subtle messages to him could have led him to some open-ended questions. He would have tried to encourage Michelle to talk more, to explain herself.

Of course, we can't blandly excuse Michelle for not being more verbally direct with Avery. Why didn't she just speak up? One of Michelle's challenges in this relationship is to recognize how important speaking up really is—and how costly it is to depend on nonverbal signals.

Costly? Yes. Nonverbal communication can be highly inflationary. That is, a wordless signal that works today may need to be doubled in intensity or dramatic appeal to work next week. A simple sigh may lose its effectiveness and must become a moan to make up the difference. A frown must turn to a scowl. Pointed avoidance inflates to flat-out isolation. These steps may start out as attempts to communicate, but once inflation takes over, they become distancers that are difficult to overcome.

Devon and Maria, on the other hand, watch for the nuances and gestures that signal escalation. They observe not in order to open up more explicit and dynamic conversation. They have no problem speaking up with vim and vigor. In fact, neither of them holds back a single passing thought or fire-building emotion. Rather, they observe to help guide and discipline their more dangerous conversations.

As you reflect on conversations in your relationship, can you identify two or three conversations that might have been improved with better observing? Imagine how talking would be different if you carefully observed every move your spouse makes. Try it.

You've come a long way already. Applying these first two elements of deep listening, to relax and to observe, has already begun to make a difference in your conversation and, therefore, in your relationship. In the next chapter we'll complete our look at listening by focusing on how opening up can help you discover things you never knew about each other, and how touch can turn trivial conversation to deep, intimate experience.

three

THE ROOT OF
LISTENING 2
OPEN UP AND TOUCH

∾

Bob and Jessica wait for their dessert and coffee after sharing a delightful dinner at Jessica's favorite bistro. As she brings up a troublesome topic, they fail to notice the imaginary auctioneer sidling up to their table.

"Bob, I'd like to talk about our spending." Jessica bites the corner of her lip, dreading Bob's inevitable shut-down. Money is a touchy subject between the two of them. By bringing it up tonight, Jessica knows she's risking an argument or possibly the silent treatment. She doesn't have long to wait.

"What for?"

"Well, I'm worried about money. I think we need to be more careful."

Bob sighs. "Okay—here we go on this again."

Our imaginary auctioneer senses things closing down quickly and wonders, *Communication going once.*

But Jessica is determined, now that she's brought it up, to see this conversation through. "I mean, it's close every month," she says, continuing. "Sometimes there's more money going out than there is coming in. I think we need a plan."

Jessica hears Bob mumble something about "checking on it" as their dessert arrives. Welcoming the diversion, Bob profusely thanks the server, and after his first big bite and gulp of coffee, he begins to talk about the excellent desserts served at this bistro. Jessica responds to his attempts at distraction with a cold stare, which sends him back to eating his pie in the mini-pout that she recognizes as his first step toward the silent treatment.

The silent auctioneer holds the gavel high as a warning. *Communication going twice.* Time passes quietly. Jessica plays with her peach cobbler, thoughtfully sips her coffee, and decides to give it one more try.

"So, about the money . . ."

Bob fakes a smile. "Are you still on that? Look—I said I'd check on it."

"Check on it? What do you mean by that? Bob, I'm totally stressing on this—I need to know what we're going to do."

Bob spoke slowly as if to a small child, his tone landing somewhere between anger and ice. "Get off it, Jess. Everything's Okay. We're fine. Quit worrying about it."

Seeing that this is going nowhere, the auctioneer slams the gavel on the table so sharply that Jessica almost hears it. *Communication sold!* he bellows. *Accusatory tone and evasive answers win yet again!* He turns his attention to another couple but stops to mutter with a wry smile, *Enjoy your cobbler.*

Some conversations open up like a daisy in the summer sun. This one snapped shut like a coffin top. Why? Clearly, Bob's cryptic, testy responses usher in the lurking auctioneer to slam down the gavel and declare an end to the bidding. And Jessica's bids to open the conversation don't seem to work. Are there hidden accusations in her seemingly innocuous words?

This clipped, emotion-packed pattern of conversation has become all too common for Bob and Jessica. Here the subject

Your Question Tool Box

Good questions are an important part of good listening. Always be on the lookout for a good question. One way to increase your mastery of questioning is to watch the masters. Choose a popular interviewer of our time, such as Larry King or Connie Chung, and watch carefully how he or she asks questions.

Which techniques connect with the character and mind of the person he or she is talking with? Which ones work best? Why? Which ones could you see yourself using on friends, colleagues, or your partner?

happened to be money and spending, but they have similar conversations about a wide range of subjects. They long for the free and flowing conversations they used to have. Where have they gone? They tend to blame their loss on the talking side of the conversation. "We don't talk the way we used to."

But open conversations develop out of good listening, not good talking. It's more about curiosity than knowing, more about questions than answers, more about receiving than giving. After all, the daisy opens to the sun not to declare its own beauty but to simply take in those warm rays. Bob and Jessica need to regain this openness with each other.

How can this be done?

By asking questions.

By simply being curious.

"Never lose a holy curiosity," said Albert Einstein. These words remind us that asking questions is a sacred art. Whether you stand, as Einstein did, before the perplexing nature of the universe or at the pulsating heart of your lover, you stand on holy ground. The conversation may focus on financial worry, simple delight at the appearance of a flower in the spring, or a strange recurring dream. You never know where your husband or wife will take you. A holy curiosity will push you to ask, to explore this strange territory. But to do so you'll need some good questions.

Good questions resemble fine tools or utensils uniquely designed to accomplish a clearly defined task. Every wood worker, for example, collects a bevy of clever and rather oddly shaped instruments specifically used to shape and join wood in ways both practical and beautiful. Every cook has a similar collection of utensils used to cut, measure, shape, cook, and serve food in ways attractive to see, smell, and taste. Good carpenters and good cooks both know the importance of having excellent, carefully maintained instruments.

Start gathering a similar collection of well-designed questions that, when asked with care and patience, will open and explore the heart and mind of the one you love. Simplicity works best. Here are a few suggestions that may work for you:

Can you give me an example of that?

How do you feel about that?

What's most important to you?

What did you like best about that?

Can you say more about that?

What would be most helpful to you right now?

Do we agree about this?

These open-ended questions lead beyond themselves and seek to uncover what lies hidden. Go back to Bob and Jessica's attempt at conversation about money, and imagine Bob asking any of the questions above. What happens? Can you see their conversation open up like a flower?

It takes only a little time and effort to notice how curiosity opens up a conversation. So begin building your own vocabulary of questions. Hundreds of beautiful, expanding questions exist. Which ones will work for you? What do you want to know about your spouse? What can you ask that most likely will keep him or her talking?

TOUCH

Touch: is there anything more beautiful, anything more exciting, anything that envelops you with more luxurious satisfaction? A simple touch can do almost anything:

Sooth you when you're upset.

Alarm you when you're complacent.

Arouse you when you're sleepy.

Make you laugh even when you're angry.

Hurt you when you least expect it.

Relax you when you're tense.

Please you when you're irritated.

Skin was earth; it was soil. I could see, even on my own skin, the joined trapezoids of dust specks God had wetted and stuck with his spit the morning he made Adam from dirt. Now, all these generations later, we people could still see on our skin the inherited prints of the dust specks of Eden.

—Annie Dillard

Annoy you when you're busy.

And that's just the beginning of the list. The possibilities for touch to help you and your partner understand each other are nearly infinite.

Why? Because there's no end to your skin. It coats your entire body. You have probably been peppered since birth with clichés that allude to the shallowness of this surface and the vanity of its appearance, but clichés only tempt us to miss the depth and meanings of skin. You may love with your heart, intuitively sense with your gut, make contact with your eye, and follow your nose. But when it comes to feeling, you feel with your skin.

Your skin, in all its sensuous wonder, carries the meanings and experiences of your life. By touching, you can activate these meanings anytime you wish. With touch you can transform your conversation from a trivial interchange into a profound connection. Deep listening recognizes the skin not only as part of the listening mechanism but also as a vital link in what it means to share all, even the deepest and most profound aspects of ourselves. Lovers know this paradise of listening skin-to-skin, where things that cannot be spoken are said.

TOUCHING TOUCHES

You can listen by touch in two ways. The first involves those times when your spouse physically touches you.

Light, casual, physical contact during conversation creates an extremely strong connection between partners. This connection keeps both of you focused on each other and on the words exchanged between you. Think, for example, about what changes occur when you touch hands across the table while talking in a restaurant. This light contact often carries distinct messages all its own.

For example, the intensity of Devon and Maria's relationship extends to the way they touch each other, which is frequent and very expressive. "Devon says a lot with his hands," says Maria. "Some people talk with their expressions, you know? They frown or smile. You can read them like a book. Devon's not like that at all. I can't always tell by looking at him what's going on with him. But with a simple touch on my arm I can tell if he's tense inside or happy, or feeling lonely or sexy."

Watching a movie together is one way to increase your familiarity with the way your partner's touch expresses emotional subtleties. A good movie will propel you through a wide range of feelings. Hold hands through a movie your partner loves but that you don't really care about. This will allow you to mentally look away from the screen and focus on the various touches that occur spontaneously as emotional experiences flash through your experience. Soon, back in reality, you'll be able to recognize meaning behind what may seem like random touches, rubs, and squeezes.

In the same way, hugging, kissing, or tickling do not usually require verbal interpretations or embellishment. The touch communicates very well on its own. In doing these things, you may murmur a verbal message to accompany the touch, but clearly the touch plays the primary role. Words play a secondary and often nonessential part. When you're hugged, you definitely know you're listening with your skin.

These listening experiences may use vast areas of your skin to communicate (the hug), or they may use extremely precise and sensitive areas (the kiss, tickling). In either case, the experiences are very strong. They can be overwhelming. They can sweep you away. In fact, research has linked these forms of touching with general health and happiness. So kiss and hug and tickle each other to your heart's content—it's good for you.

The 10 by 10

Choose a time when the two of you can be alone and undisturbed for 30 to 45 minutes. For the first 10 minutes talk freely to your partner about anything you like. Your partner will listen to you, using all the techniques of deep listening found in the ROOT method.

When 10 minutes have passed, switch roles for the next 10 minutes.

You listen while your partner talks about anything except what you were talking about.

Make this switch two or three times. Allow yourselves 10 or 15 minutes at the end of your time to reflect on your listening experiences. Do this regularly, and you'll soon find these habits of good listening appearing naturally in your normal conversation.

TOUCHLESS TOUCHES

What about touches that don't touch? Gestures illustrate or amplify spoken words by copying the motions of touch without any actual physical contact. Gestures touch you from a distance. With gestures, your partner can rub you, soothe you, hug you, kiss you, or dismiss you, all in midair while your skin tells you how it all feels.

For example, when Devon wants to make a point he feels strongly about, he gives the table a quick, hard rap with his fist. He believes his gesture simply expresses his passion for what he's saying. Maria, however, feels differently about this gesture. To her, it's a violent gesture that makes her skin tighten in defense every single time it happens. Listening to his words becomes impossible at that point, and communication breaks down.

This confuses them both. Neither one thinks that the gesture carries a threat. Devon has never hit Maria. But while she knows that intellectually, her skin tells her something different—not, perhaps, that Devon would hit her, but that hitting is dangerous. Either way, she can't listen to Devon because she hears something in that gesture that overrides his words. Until they find a solution, their conversations end at the point when things matter most to Devon.

The effects that touch and gestures have on us demonstrate the importance of listening with your skin. Maria shows remarkable self-awareness and courage when she refuses to ignore her skin's message to her. In the same way, your skin not only helps you hear your partner but also constantly reflects back to you your own feelings. Your skin tells you what is going on. Every sensation has a message. Creeping skin says disgust. Warm skin usually speaks of safety or security. Tightening skin registers fear. Goose bumps show chill or coldness, while flushing and blushing signal embarrassment. Tingling skin demonstrates arousal or excitement.

Your skin, touch, and gestures play a major role in your listening process. As the largest organ of your body, your skin hears messages and meanings from your partner while also helping to clarify your own sometimes clouded responses.

In summary, follow the course of the ROOT—relax, observe, open up, and touch. Listening that grows from this root involves more than simply holding down one side of a conversation. All that's deepest and best about being human can be touched and affirmed through an authentic and profound act of listening.

section two
LIGHT TALK

How much time do couples need together to create a lasting, bonded marriage? Obviously, wide individual differences exist, but daily contact is needed by most couples. Couples who find one hour each day to be together have adopted one of the most potent, therapeutic marital aids.
—Linda Berg-Cross

And God said, "Let there be light."
—Gen. 1:3

four

THE UNBEARABLE
LOSS OF LIGHTNESS

❧

The Book of Genesis opens like a bad dream. A chaotic mass of shapeless and formless goo swirls before you like sludge in a bottomless pit. In your worst nightmare, the goo-filled pit beckons you. It draws you closer and closer despite your terror. You can't resist its power as it slowly sucks you in. You have nothing to stop it, nothing to slow you down, nothing to hold onto. The force of this chaos draws you ineluctably to the rim of its pit. Kicking and screaming, you feel the earth giving way beneath you. You start to fall.

At this point in the nightmare, you're begging yourself to wake up. Your marriage partner, startled by your screams and a bit miffed at your kicking in bed, shakes you with one hand, reaches to turn on the bedside light with the other, and cries "Wake up! Wake up!"

That's exactly what happens in Gen. 1:3 when God, whose Spirit had been hovering nearby, finally speaks. "And God said, 'Let there be light', and there was light." Nightmares usually end when the light goes on. In our worst moments of darkness

Connection Time

Set a definite time for connection. With your busy schedules, light talk can be roughly shouldered out of the daily flow of life. If you wait for connection to happen by itself, you'll probably never see it happen. Take matters into your own hands by agreeing to sit back for at least 10 or 15 minutes every day to unwind, connect, and relax together. Setting a definite time and place will keep it from slipping away.

and fright, we crave the light. It helps us separate, as God did, day from night, order from chaos, tranquility from fear.

Natalie and Dominic are falling into just such a nightmare after 11 years of marriage. On the outside things look fine. Both work hard and competently at their jobs. Natalie is a customer service supervisor in a department store, while Dominic is a city firefighter. But back at home, life is falling apart. Aimee, Natalie's 14-year-old daughter from a brief first marriage, seems suddenly addicted to boys, troubled friends, and loud, late-night cell phone conversations. When Dominic confronts Aimee, their conversations explode into intense screaming matches.

Meanwhile, their two youngest children, Toby and Jeanne, are struggling with their work at school, and it's becoming clear that each of them has some significant developmental and learning problems. They're falling behind academically and socially and require a flood of attention in the way of parent-teacher meetings, parental help, psychiatric appointments, and remedial therapy.

As the pressure of family life grows stronger, the call for clear communication and cooperation between Natalie and Dominic increases. Misunderstandings and scheduling breakdowns lead to missed appointments, irate children, and mutual blaming. Mealtime chaos and the ensuing arguments drive a wedge between them like an ax in a pine stump. They both know something needs to be done. Somehow they need to get their house in order. But when do they have time to work on it? And what is it that actually needs to be done?

The Genesis nightmare of shapeless chaos haunts their home. "This is not the way to raise children," groans Dominic, but he also knows it's not a way to be married. They start to talk about splitting up, not because they have a better solution but because neither can stand the tension and fighting anymore.

Natalie sums it up: "The more we try, the harder we work,

the more distant we become. Sometimes it feels like it's not just our marriage—our whole world is splitting apart."

What world is Natalie talking about? It's the world that she and Dominic are trying to create together. It seemed to be going according to plan, but now it's teetering on the brink of failure. She and Dominic are desperately groping in the darkness for the light switch. Where is it?

The move from chaos to order, from distance to connection, enters your marriage through a certain kind of conversation called light talk. It's interesting to note in the passage from Genesis that light appeared when God spoke, suggesting the very intimate and profound connection between shared words and saving light. In the same way, when your way grows dark, you need words that bring the light of clarity, connection, and joy back into your relationship. You need light talk.

Light talk is to marriage what the trunk is to a tree. Both provide the essential connection, structure, and protection necessary for life and health. No marriage can survive the loss of light talk.

LET THERE BE LIGHT TALK

While its name suggests cheerfulness, light talk addresses some of the most basic and important aspects of life together. It's the talk that connects, as the trunk connects the parts of an apple tree. A loss of connective conversation between partners almost always involves a breakdown in the order of life. Things start going wrong. Days start falling apart. Chaos creeps in and makes itself at home at your kitchen table. The loss of connection brings turbulence. Nobody knows who is supposed to do what task or when to do it. Insecurity about what's happening shoots up like a roman candle.

This is not the way you want to live. You didn't marry to create chaos and distance but rather to be close and connected.

Blended Worlds

Blending two worlds into one is hard work. Be sure that you're talking enough about the two worlds you live in. Occasionally reverse positions when you talk. Have your partner talk to you about your world—your daily tasks, the people you spend time with, your annoyances and frustrations—for about 15 minutes. Then switch roles and talk about 15 minutes about your partner's world.

So instead of living that bad dream, let there be light talk. What kind of conversation is light talk? How will it provide these qualities in your marriage? It may surprise you how easy, how weightless, how smooth light talk can be. You're already highly skilled but perhaps rather neglectful in light talk.

Consider this. When you discuss the weather or your plans for a picnic, you're light talking. When you report to each other the ups and downs of the day, you're light talking. Responding to a report on the news, making a quick phone call in the middle of the day just to touch base, laughing together about your young child's antics, coordinating your weekly schedules—these are a few out of hundreds of examples of light talk you use every day.

So let there be light talk! Spend more time talking together. Carve out time each day to relax and connect with your partner. Just be yourselves together. Finding that time can be a challenge, of course. Linda Berg-Cross, in the quote that begins this section, suggests that couples find one hour each day to spend together. That may seem like a pipe dream to you, but why not try? Every second you spend lightly with your partner is worth its weight in gold in relational rewards. Think of what would happen in just a month if you and your partner spent more time talking:

More time laughing.

More time musing and amusing one another.

More time coordinating your busy schedules.

More time exchanging daily reports.

More time checking in and catching up.

More time smiling, joking, chatting, goofing around.

More time teasing, gossiping, escaping.

More time hugging and squeezing.

More time dating and mating.

Right now you probably spend less time doing all the fun stuff you vowed you would never get away from. You hate to say it, but your marriage is beginning to look a little like that of your parents. (Sorry to bring that up.) So create some of that time together. Start talking. Soon you'll find your light conversation taking as many shapes and forms as there are types of tree tunks in a forest.

Let there be light talk.

From the breathtaking splendor of the California redwood to the slender grace of the New Hampshire birch, the tree trunk demonstrates the beauty and importance of connection. Some trunks tower tall enough to reach the sky. Others bring a smile as they scoot, stout and stubby, along the ground. The tree trunk takes many forms and shapes, always balancing the blueprint of its species with the pressures of its environment.

In whatever shape, the trunk serves important functions for the tree. It provides the basic structure upon which the rest of the tree grows. It also connects the various parts of the tree, channeling the moisture and nutrients from soil to branches, leaves, and fruit. Finally a protective layer of bark keeps these important inner processes safe from outside forces and disease. The purposes of light talk, like those of the tree trunk, include connection, structure, and protection.

CONNECTION: THE TWO SHALL BE ONE

Like you and your partner, Natalie and Dominic spend most of their active waking hours apart. Natalie comes home exhausted from a day dealing with the complaints, pressures, and anger of disgruntled customers. She's looking for an evening of few demands, quiet conversation, and relaxation. But she also brings some of those tensions home with her and needs to air them, vent a little about them, and even laugh about them.

Dominic deals with daily pressures of a different sort. After a day of danger, trying to avert disaster, and adrenaline overdose, he comes home ready to eat, sleep, and revive himself. But

Time to Date

When did you last go out on a date? Dating, you may recall, was all about light talk most of the time. Going out for fun regularly brings the lightness and connection back into your relationship.

he also has experiences that he needs to share—stories of close calls or firehouse boredom that he needs to process with someone. And, of course, each job is riddled with workplace politics and relational stresses that don't destroy the love each has for the job but sometimes get in the way of enjoying it. For Natalie and Dominic, as for most couples, these work environments comprise different worlds.

Other than conversation, what can bring these worlds together? Without plenty of light talk, you'll feel the separation of your parallel lives. Relationship fade begins as these important segments of experience and meaning slowly evaporate from your common world and remain isolated in the mind and experience of both of you separately.

Instead of allowing your relationship to fade like this, be sure that you know in general what's going on in your partner's day. Talk about it briefly when you part, and then follow up with a debriefing time when you join again later. You need to know the challenges and personalities that inhabit the world of your partner, perhaps not fully and deeply known, but known nonetheless. Who are the major players? What are they like? What are they up to? Minute details may not be necessary or desired, but talking in this light, relaxed way creates a common existence. By talking, you take the various strands of your separate lives and weave a common cloth together.

The strands of life that you're weaving together relate not just to work. You also want to share matters that have to do with extended family, interests, friends, and community events.

Couples who share their worlds with each other feel far more connected than those who do not. Light talk builds a common world. When you share your day's experiences, laugh together at something that happened to one of you, learn by report the ebb and flow of your partner's life, you're making two worlds one.

STRUCTURE: DANCE WITH ME

Have you ever sat back at a wedding reception and watched the couples dance? It can be quite entertaining. You may notice one couple who seems to have it totally together. They flow across the floor in perfect sync with each other. The complexity of their dance seems to flow out of their bodies with the grace of a loping gazelle.

Right next to them on the floor you may see another couple straining and struggling to get their steps right. They clutch each other and move stiffly back and forth, trying to be sure they do it right. They seem to be mumbling to each other and smile occasionally when one steps on the other's foot. This couple is never showy, never flashy, but they get the job done.

Then along come the wild ones. Totally energized and carefree, moving with no discernable patterns or dance steps, this couple is just having fun. In their wild and unpredictable movements, they occasionally create a risk for other dancers who venture too close to their dancing whirlwind. But everybody really loves to watch this couple dance.

In fact, all three couples are having fun. They just each dance in their own style.

In the same way, your life dance requires structure, and different styles of life require different types of order. If you both work full-time jobs outside the home, you place certain demands on the organization of your home. A couple in which one or both are in military service will find their life together will need to respond to the structure inherent in that way of life. Families who have chosen to school their children at home face unique challenges in structure. External structures, such as jobs and environment, place demands on your ability to create and maintain the internal structures that sustain love and happiness. The interplay of externally imposed and internally developed structures creates one of the most fascinating dances of marriage.

To List or Not to List—That Is the Question.

Many couples include one partner who loves lists and uses reams of paper to order the process of getting things done. The other partner claims to carry a list of things to do "in my head," a tactic difficult to distinguish from having no list at all.

Is one of you a list-maker? How do the two of you relate to each other around that list? Does the list create tension between you? How can your differences in this area become smoother and more effective?

Becoming a couple means you've stepped on the dance floor. You may embark on life in the suburbs, an urban center, or choose a wild, country place. Wherever you go, you'll find the dance waiting. How will you organize your life together? How will the structure you freely create together relate to the structures imposed by the demands and characteristics of the careers you've each chosen?

The basic structure of your home revolves around four essential needs of life: eating, sleeping, working, and playing. When you decide how these essentials are going to take place, you've created an outline, a frame, a trunk on which the rest of your life can be built. This trunk needs to be strong enough to hold everything up yet flexible enough to bend a little when the winds blow.

Couples vary from one extreme to the other in determining what level of order works best for them. Some couples choose to be quite rigid while others tend to be almost chaotic. In the end, all couples find some way of lending order to their lives and to their relationship.

In the day-to-day flow of life, light talk meets the need for structure. Most daily tasks, shifts, changes, and duties can be handled well with light conversations. Communicating about which of you will handle certain tasks, where you'll be, what you'll be doing, what you need, when you'll call, what you can pick up at the store, where you'll meet for coffee—these communications structure the day. Of course, the day may not go as planned. They seldom do. But the basic outline is there to give confidence, coordination, and direction to your actions.

PROTECTION: GOOD FENCES

The tree trunk continues its amazing service to the tree by providing a protective coating around itself. Bark ensures that the onslaught of the outside world never gets inside to disrupt

Checking the Flow of Life

At least once a month, go over together the daily flow of your lives. Are tasks being handled efficiently? Are chores being done? Does the arrangement of responsibilities seem fair to both of you? Are any changes anticipated? Basically, are you living life on the same page?

the processes and structures so vital to the life of the tree. The texture, style, and color of bark vary greatly from tree to tree, but its purpose is always to protect.

Light talk helps provide a clear protective boundary around your relationship. That boundary keeps the outside world from getting in. Imagine the boundary around you as a dotted line or as a picket fence. You keep certain people, forces, and pressures out, effectively preventing them from messing up what you have together. Like bark, this boundary guards against intrusive influence.

At the same time, this boundary contains and protects that which you wish to keep inside the realm of your relationship. Most couples agree to keep certain secrets, struggles, or ideas strictly between the two of them. This boundary helps create the feeling of safety and trust necessary for a growing intimacy.

Light talk sometimes actually forms this fence around you. You've often observed a happy couple in a restaurant or on a park bench. They talk, laugh, and make nearly continual eye contact. The rest of us cease to exist. They're in their own world. Most often these couples are not sharing deep and profound emotional realities. More likely, they're reviewing the day's activities, sharing something they read in a magazine, talking lightly about a family member or friend, or just sharing a laugh about one of their own idiosyncrasies. The warmth that surrounds a couple talking this way creates a feeling of homey, hearth-like intimacy and goodness. Light talk carries this hearth wherever it goes. The portable hearth of light talk enables you to feel safe and protected anywhere.

In order to provide these benefits in your life, light talk follows certain basic guidelines. Light talk remains light talk only when you follow the rules for talking and listening. Chapter five outlines these guidelines for you along the acronyms BODY and TRUNK. Have fun!

five

CREATING YOUR
TOGETHER WORLD

∾

The guidelines for talking and listening in light talk are relatively simple. They emphasize the relaxed framework intended for this mode of conversation. You know you're light talking when you feel relaxed and connected. This form of conversation is often linked with certain places: the kitchen, the hearth, or the table. These places stand in the middle of the swirl of life. They're where your basic needs get met, such as food, shelter, and a sense of belonging. These needs play an essential role in your health and are usually accompanied by a consistent flow of positive light talk. Gather family and friends around a table, and light talk is apt to appear.

Couples share this talking in a wide variety of circumstances and levels of intensity. Light talk is a mood as much as a style of conversation—a mood of languid, indescribable, sensuous pleasure. The following guidelines for talking and listening in light talk are simply ways to extend and enjoy that mood.

TALKING

Being the one talking in light talk can be among the most relaxing and enjoyable activities of your day. You already spend hours engaged in light talk every week. Some of that time you're talking with friends, some with acquaintances at work, while other valuable time is spent in light talk with your spouse. When you talk in this mode, remember that you're in the dimension of the BODY: bend, organize, debrief, and yak.

BEND

Expect interruptions and quick subject changes during light talk. This kind of talk often resembles a game of tag. First one and then the other is "it." Conversation happens with light exchanges and playful banter, punctuated with smatterings of laughter. The attention span in light talk is short, so don't allow interruptions or rapid shifts to irritate you or create problems. Flexibility allows your light talk to ramble and wander and respond to the ideas and suggestions of your partner. Always be ready to move on.

Light talk often reminds me of popping corn. As the heat increases, there's a flurry of activity. A wild cacophony ensues that defies any attempt to analyze or understand it. Like popping kernels of corn, the conversation bounces back and forth from one to the other. No topic is followed through. No idea is pursued. One story follows another in rapid fire. Sometimes one story is interrupted by another and must be completed later on. Then gradually things slow down. A more relaxed tone fills the room. Such talking requires a high level of flexibility from both partners as the conversation bends and pops from topic to topic.

ORGANIZE

One of the primary tasks in light talk involves organizing your life together. Setting up the routine, connecting about ever-changing daily tasks and errands, and being sure that the flow of your life retains a sense of order and predictability all require regular conversation. Failure to consistently engage in organizing light talk means that miscommunications and frustrating slip-ups keep occurring. As we saw briefly with Natalie and Dominic, alarming and frustrating events may occur: important appointments missed, children not picked up on time, or bills left unpaid. These breakdowns may be just the tip of the iceberg of chaos that begins to eat away at the security of your life together.

The organizing part of light talk requires talking about schedules, chores, responsibilities, and errands that help keep your home life flowing in an ordered, connected, and comforting way.

DEBRIEF

As noted above, on most days you and your partner probably spend more time apart than together. Jobs, family responsibilities, friends, and recreation often pull you in opposite directions. In order to prevent these pressures that can tear apart the fabric of your relationship, you both need to debrief each other on what has happened.

How was your day?

How did it go at the doctor's?

How was your flight?

What's going on over at your mother's house?

Questions such as these open the door for a brief, informed update. Unless more serious issues lurk beneath these questions, debriefing is usually a lighthearted, low-pressure sharing of what you've experienced in the time you've spent apart.

YAK

Light talk lets you be who you are. It expresses you at your informal best. Often it follows your mind as you wander from topic to topic, from place to place. You make jokes, you tease, you comment on a politician all in the span of a moment or two. Light talk, whether it happens at home or somewhere else, catches you with your slippers on. When talking in this mode, let it flow. Highly structured, goal-oriented ideas seem strange and out of place. Relax and let yourself flow.

In this way, safety plays an important role in light talk. Designed to be relaxing, it can function only in an atmosphere of trust and care. No one likes to settle in for a quiet conversation and get hit with deep emotional turmoil or accusations. Your listening partner will begin to lose trust in the sacred space of intimate light talk if you continue to ambush the feeling of relaxation with gut-wrenching experiences or intricate problems.

Bob and Jessica wrestle with time to yak. Bob's personality expresses itself in light talk, and Jessica knows that it's being generously given to others while she gets only the leftovers. She wants to see his charming, humorous self again and realizes that to find that they need to find time together. They begin by setting up a regular Tuesday lunch appointment. They guard that time ferociously from interference by other demands while they also keep themselves away from weighted or sensitive topics. "It's our time to chit-chat" Bob explains. "We can't live without it."

Saving the heavy talks for later and giving clear indication when you need to shift gears from light to heavy-duty conversation will help keep light talk feeling safe and set up the heavier conversation for success later on. Prolonged arguments, impassioned pleas, and complex story lines require different types of conversing styles. In light talk you make simple observations, stab a quick point home, or throw an idea against the wall to see if it sticks. When complexity begins to edge into your conversation, it may be a sign that you need to move to a different style.

LISTENING

Light talk listening demands somewhat less concentration than other modes of conversation. The casual nature of light talk often allows the listener to participate in something else. Preparing a meal together, walking, traveling, and gardening: these activities can all be enjoyed accompanied by light conversation. Sustained eye contact and focused posture are not required. The act of listening in this case involves caring interest without intense digging. This mode of conversation seeks connection, not depth.

Because light talk listening serves to protect the mood and boundaries of the connective link between you, your style needs to follow this simple outline of the TRUNK: track, relax, understand, no lectures, and keep on.

TRACK

The first rule in light-talk listening is to pay attention. The temptation to allow your attention to drift to other things can be very strong. The subject matter may not always be exactly enthralling, and minimizing its importance can become habitual. But as in architecture, so it is with well-constructed relationships; God is in the details.

The crucial role of light talk in your relationship insists that you track your partner's talking with close attention. As we have seen, light talk provides the connection and protection you both need. Its many tasks include the ongoing structure of your life together. It's a gift indeed that these important aspects of relationship center on a style of conversation that for the most part is light and cheerful. But never let the lightness compromise the importance of listening to the details of life. Focusing attention on these many details in lightly talking speaks elegantly of your commitment to the nurture of your relationship and to the value you place on the flow of your life together.

RELAX

The ability of the listener to relax complements the speakers call to bend and be flexible. Light talk resembles those changing fountains you've seen in the mall or at the park. The water sprays up in ever-changing formations and combinations, while lights of various colors add depth and feeling to your experience. Talking lightly with each other, you move through a similar range of subjects and moods. The unique aspect about light talk rests in the fact that you never stay too long on any one subject or mood. The conversation constantly shifts, and as the listener, you must follow.

The splash of your voices, the freedom to chatter, and the experience of unrestricted flow between you lend stability and pleasure. In light talk the process of conversation matters as much as the content. Many couples use light talk as a way to unwind at the end of the day. Breathe deeply and allow the stress to leave you. Relax as you listen. Gracefully go with the flow.

UNDERSTAND

The lightness characteristic of this style of conversation does not absolve a listener from the supreme task of all listening: to understand. Take in all your marriage partner is saying in both the organizing and the debriefing aspects. Important events and experiences slip into light talk, and the consistent and caring listener latches on to them like a steel trap. The informality and fun of connecting becomes a false front if important information is allowed to escape unheard.

Often very important information is exchanged through light talk. From the needed gallon of milk to the scheduled doctor's appointment, light talk helps you keep things going. Failing to attend properly usually means something is going to fall apart. Light talk doesn't require depth analysis, high levels of prolonged concentration, gut-wrenching disclosures, or spirited confrontations. But it does insist on simple attention.

Listen lightly, but listen well.

NO LECTURES

Perhaps the most important guideline for listening in light talk is the prohibition against heaviness. Don't advise, solve, pontificate, or exhibit any other form of serious intention. Just listen. These heavy responses have their places in other forms of conversation, but they mess things up in light talk.

Let friendship be your guide. Light talk is a hallmark of friendship, and listening as a friend usually omits somber, advisory responses unless they're specifically asked for. Your partner often needs you to listen in this way, as a friend.

KEEP ON

Light talk remains one of the most significant aspects of couple conversation simply because, if done regularly and well, it's just plain fun. It provides time for you to enjoy each other in the context of a very limited agenda. The more time you can spend together in this relaxed atmosphere, the more connected and comfortable your relationship will become.

Light talk is to conversation what a country drive is to traveling. With no particular place to go, no responsibilities to fulfill, no plans or ideas to realize, you're free to relax. Never underestimate the importance of doing nothing together. As a listener, try to stretch these times to their maximum. Keep on listening for more.

The style of conversation called light talk, like a warm fire, usually feels very nice. You and your partner will ultimately decide on a level of closeness and connection that works best for you and that provides what you both want and need in your relationship. Using light talk along these guidelines will help you provide the structure vital to maintaining a healthy and connected relationship. Chapter six explores some ways that you can use the five senses to enhance and enrich your light talk with variety, interest, and sensuality.

six

SENSUOUS CONVERSATION

Michelle remained concerned and confused about her marriage. She and Avery had been married two years now. They had recovered from their honeymoon disaster, but things had begun to slip away from her. Avery approached his life the same way he had approached their honeymoon: planning the schedule of activities and then exhausting them both trying to work the plan. They weren't fighting much, but Michelle felt distant, disconnected.

Early one June morning she quietly slid open the glass door and slipped from the kitchen onto the deck overlooking her backyard. She was determined to make sense of her marriage. *What's happening? What's going wrong? Why do I feel so distant and disconnected from Avery?*

She stretched her legs, snuggled comfortably back in her chair and, wrapping her fingers around the warm cup, took a long sip of coffee, savoring its rich, tart taste. The flavor blended nicely with the smell of the morning dew-moist grass, newly mowed the day before. A bird's song drew her attention to the young maple in the corner of the yard where leaves fluttered noisily in the soft morning breeze.

If only, she thought, *if only marriage were this easy. If only we were into each other the way I'm now into this summer morning.* She let her mind wander with these thoughts. *How? Totally. Wonderfully. Physically.* She stretched her legs again and took another sip and leaned back with eyes closed. "Sensuously," she whispered. Her eyes popped open. "That's it!" she said it out loud. "Sensuously!"

She relished the turn of meaning of the word "sense" as she came to her senses. *It's not making sense of marriage but making sense in marriage that matters.*

Michelle turned this idea slowly over and over in her mind. She reflected that her conversations with Avery were often saturated with ideas and problems, but they seldom reveled in the sheer sensuousness of life. They didn't share moments like this on the deck because they really didn't have a conversational style that fits with sipping coffee, listening to a breeze, and smelling a new-mowed lawn. Michelle decided right then to change that. She headed for the bedroom, determined to drag him outside for some sumptuous conversation. She smiled as she passed the little sign she had posted over the coffee pot a few weeks before: "Wake up and smell the coffee!"

The conversation Michelle was pointing at is sensuous conversation. It's filled to the brim with light talk. It lightly and deftly restores connection by centering on the five senses your body uses to make the physical world feel real and important. Restoring the connection to each other and to the world you're creating together involves reconnecting with the senses that make it live. Sensuousness breeds conversation. To revitalize your light talk, join Avery and Michelle and plunge deeply into the sensuous world by using the five pathways of sense.

TOUCH

The appreciation and practice of touch in your relationship

will bring rich dividends in the health of your relationship and, as research continues to show, in your personal health as well. Touches of nearly every form and description can be used to form a bond of safety and connection as you talk. Light talk is bound to happen if the two of you simply touch. Simply reach out and hold hands while traveling in the car. Snuggle while you watch a movie. Let your legs entwine themselves as you relax on the couch. As mentioned earlier, your skin, the medium of touch, covers you completely, so the sensation of touching each other can happen in the most common and serendipitous ways. Allow it to happen, and revel in the sensuous pleasure of it.

Some forms of touch can also be done with a specific purpose in mind. Touching in the form of back-rubs, massages, or tickling has distinct intentions such as relaxation, stress management, playfulness, or as steps toward lovemaking. Other forms of touching are subtler and serve to create an environment of comfort and familiarity. The textures and surfaces you come in contact with while you talk can be very important to a relaxed, soothing conversation. Being comfortable, that is, having your skin and body in contact with surfaces that are pleasurable, will greatly aid the play of light talk.

TASTE

Taste can also enrich your experience of light talk. The point has previously been made that food often triggers relaxed, connected conversation. Tasting things together, and enjoying that fun and pleasure, can unlock doors and bring down the barriers of stress and anxiety that prevent light talk from occurring.

Tasting and the sensations that go with it are meant to be relaxing. Designed as part of the way to relieve the hunger drive, taste satisfies and connects. The habit that so many couples share of gobbling food in front of the television night after night represents a tragic loss in relationship.

So allow taste to provide a pathway to talk. Prepare foods that you both enjoy. Experimenting with your taste buds can be a true and enjoyable way of exploring ways to talk together. Try something new, and see what you end up talking about. And, of course, few experiences match the cozy conversations you have when you return to familiar foods and the tastes you've shared together time and time again. Make tasting a ceremony, not because you worship food but because it opens an excitingly sensuous door to bright, fun, stress-relieving conversation.

Another way to use taste to encourage the use of light talk between you is to expand the numbers of tasters. Dining together with friends or other family members almost guarantees that a healthy dose of light talk will pour out as plentiful and enjoyable as the food. If you as a couple have forgotten how to connect, eating with friends can help remind you of the joys and fun you used to have together.

SIGHT

Seeing also contributes to good light talk. Your eyes constantly take in your surroundings, allowing your brain to make judgments. Some input creates tension and stress, while another produces relaxation. What you see can be alarming or soothing. To create space for light talk, consider the things your eyes will take in as you speak.

As you try to build an environment for talking to take place, be mindful of the pleasure felt by viewing certain colors and objects. As most of your relaxed talking will take place in your home, creating rooms that look relaxing and soothing can help your conversation to mirror those feelings.

Use art, pictures, colors, and windows to bring about this atmosphere. Generally, organization feels more relaxing than chaos, so an orderly home works better for most couples. Of course, being too rigid about order can produce a sense of rigidity and expectations than tend to increase tension. Each couple must find the balance in organization that works for them. The point here is that each of you, in order to spark your interest in small talk, needs to feel comfortable upon walking into your home. That first positive visual impression helps fan that spark.

It's also good to change the scenery from time to time. Going on walks opens different sights and vistas to the eyes and makes the connection between you easy. Taking a trip together does the same thing in a grander scale. These are ways of using your eyes, your gift of sight, to enhance your relationship by providing atmospheres contributory to good talking.

Seeing also includes the way you truly and refreshingly look at each other. How do the two of you see each other? How much time each day do you devote to the seeing part of your relationship? Focusing on your partner with your knowing and accepting eyes of love can constantly provide new perspectives, greater understanding, and a deeper appreciation. Looking at the body, the movements, the gestures, the eyes of your partner, yields a sense of what's happening there and provides a complement to the deeper sort of seeing that involves direct eye-to-eye contact. Look and see.

Your looking also creates in your partner that wonderful and necessary sense of being seen, an awareness of your sight. The desire to be seen, that is, of not being invisible or ignored, claws at the heart of us all just as deeply and savagely as the desires to be heard, to be touched, or to be included. Give to each other generously the gift of being seen.

HEARING

Your sense of hearing, of course, has many practical and useful purposes. Some of these were discussed in the chapter on deep listening. In using this particular pathway for connection, however, focus on using your ears to give you a sense of wonder and flow in the larger context of life, and use that wonder to seal your connection to each other.

The contribution of hearing to light talk provides a deep grounding and connection to your immediate environment and through that to life itself. Your relationship can feel richly embedded in the flow of life as you accept the sounds that surround you.

If you have children, you need no introduction to the sounds of life. They cry, they squabble, they laugh. They scream, ask innumerable questions, and tell innumerable stories. They bump, they run, they slam, they jump—all these after you've asked them to please be quiet. It may be against these sounds of life that you and your partner try to connect.

Other life sounds can also provide a backdrop for light talk. The muffled chatting of 15 conversations in a crowded restaurant chants the tune of life. The music of the birds in your backyard singing to each other on a summer morning chimes the music of life. The wind driving rain against your window, the hum of traffic with its occasional blare of horns, the cry of the loon on a distant northern lake—all connect you aurally to the pulse of industry and life that beats around you and in you.

When you and your partner pause together to allow such sounds to flood your togetherness, you receive that pleasure that comes with knowing your deep connection with all that is. Your own playful conversation acts as a descant over this marvelous symphony of sound.

In creating your hearing space for light talk, you'll probably need to ban certain sounds. Listening to the birds can't happen with the television set blaring out the morning news or the radio marching out the top 40. Protect the soundscape of your light talk as vigorously and as discriminatingly as you protect your sight from ugly scenes and your taste from insipid soup.

SMELL

The sense of smell provides the final connection to the sensuous world. Aroma can serve to ground you in a place of peace and the expectation of connection. Smells that relate to other senses can be doubly powerful. Some smells connect with taste. The smell of a meal cooking or of fresh brewed coffee can trigger the thoughts of connection, relaxation, satisfaction, and talking. The smell of the scented oil you use to massage your partner's back brings thoughts of touching, while the smell of fresh rain brings anticipation of the bird's song. The aromas that surround you can all be used to help ground you in your body and help you connect with your partner on that level.

Purposefully use smell to signal a relaxed and connected time and space for you and your partner by lighting a scented candle or opening a window to let in the fresh morning air. When done regularly, these aromas can lead you and your partner into the good habit of connection.

Also of note here is the actual personal smell you carry to your partner. There's power in the way you smell. When you're clean or sweaty, when you're wearing perfume or cologne, when you bring the odors that cling to you after a day at work, all these smells send subtle but powerful messages back and forth to each other. The medium of aroma can be a wonderful addition to your ability to connect conversationally in this relaxed and physically based way.

This very rapid trip through the senses is intended to set you free. You'll find that you have certain senses that are particularly strong for you. Perhaps your ears are sensitive to certain sounds. Maybe your nose picks up smells others miss, and these smells carry the ability to sweep you away. You don't need to be equally as acute in all five senses—very few people are. You have your stronger and weaker senses as does your partner. Find that information out and use it to help you connect.

Volumes have been written on the senses. Some write from a scientific viewpoint, while others from a more experiential stance. Learn what you can about how they work, and use that to develop an ever-strengthening bond between you and your spouse on this very strong, important, and exciting aspect of your relationship.

section three
MIND TALK

Make my joy complete by being like-minded.
—Phil. 2:2

Owing to heredity, early training, or, in all probability, a constant interaction between these factors, some individuals will develop certain intelligences far more than others; but every normal individual should develop each intelligence to some extent, given but a modest opportunity to do so.
—Howard Gardner

seven

PROBLEMS, PUZZLES, AND POSSIBILITIES

❧

"Sometimes I hear the words you say, but I just don't understand where you're coming from."

Dominic and Natalie are arguing about how to handle Natalie's teenaged daughter, Aimee. Aimee doesn't like her new curfew and has consistently been staying out past the hour she's expected home. For Dominic it's a simple matter. There are rules established, and everyone needs to abide by those rules or face the consequences. "If you say 11 o'clock, then she needs to be here at 11 o'clock," he insists. "Not 11:05. Not 11:15. Certainly not 12:30, like it was last night."

Dominic points to the fact that everyone in the house has rules. Everyone has a schedule. He needs to be at work at 7 o'clock every morning. What if he started showing up an hour late? "Would my boss put up with that? Would I have a job tomorrow? Aimee needs to learn some of life's realities."

Dominic is not shy about turning this problem back on Natalie. He thinks that Aimee's "rebellion" is fueled by Natalie's "squishy-soft" approach. "If you get tough, she'll straighten out—guaranteed!"

Natalie has a different take. She sees her 16-year-old daughter struggling with a lot of issues. Aimee spends alternate weekends with her father and his new wife, Diane, whose quiet and structured home contrasts sharply with the near chaos that unfolds daily at what Natalie calls the dinner-homework-bedtime sequence. Aimee calls it "Camp Dominic."

Starting as soon as they get home and working their way through the entire "sequence," Aimee's two younger siblings fight, cry, pitch fits, throw toys, refuse food, splash bathwater, and wage raucous pillow fights. Dominic marches around the house after them like a wind-up drill sergeant. He barks orders, threatens dire consequences, and acts like the man in charge but retreats into a sorry pout when his efforts are ignored, as they consistently are. Natalie tries to instill some order into that chaos but refuses to out-shout Dominic and soon retreats to her bedroom and pajamas, emerging long enough to kiss the kids good-night when the pillow fight has ended.

Natalie knows that Aimee just wants to get out of there. Aimee hates the chaos and further suspects that the new curfew is the brainchild of her stepfather, not her mother. Aimee sees no reason and has no desire to bend to his wishes.

In addition to this, Natalie recognizes that Aimee's involvement with Sean, her first boyfriend, is a factor. Though Natalie understands this relationship will run its course and end after a brief span, Aimee is convinced that she's hopelessly and eternally in love. Every minute she spends with Sean is an investment in their future. Natalie is afraid that if she suddenly gets too strict with Aimee, she may lose touch with her relationally. "She may just cut me off, just like I did with my mother when I was her age. I don't want that to happen." Considering the consequences, Natalie in no way wants to flirt with that danger at this point in Aimee's life.

Natalie is not being emotional, as Dominic claims when she brings up her concerns. She's very thoughtful, but her thinking takes note of Aimee's inner dynamics. Dominic's thinking is more rule-oriented and structured. They're both thinking hard, trying to solve this problem together, but they don't seem willing or able to understand each other. Their minds work differently.

That's why they've both exclaimed with a sigh, "Sometimes I hear the words you say, but I just don't understand where you're coming from."

MINDS THAT MEET

What is the mind? Is it the deeply spiritual process Buddhists refer to as mindfulness? Does it involve the technological wonder of artificial intelligence? Will mind talk lead us to consider the differences between your mind and your brain? The wonder of consciousness? No, no, and no. We're here using mind in its most direct and experiential meaning. Your mind is what you use to think, and mind talk is how you express your thoughts with each other.

Intelligent synchronicity is as significant a measure of intimacy as emotional closeness. Many couples judge their relationship by how they feel or how they share their feelings. Feelings are important, but a couple must become as adept at expressing and analyzing their thoughts as they are willing to share and affirm their feelings. The unfolding of your relationship in the flux and flow of everyday life demands a meeting of the minds. It's not so you'll think alike. That's a goal both unattainable and undesirable. You don't want to think alike—you want to understand what and how each other thinks.

A successful meeting of the minds between you and your partner will involve a healthy and loving respect for the nature and capacities of each other's intelligence. When you value the intellectual gifts of one above the other, you not only create frustration and anger but also short circuit any problem-solving method you've developed. Life together is too complex and var-

Practice in Brainstorming

Select an area of your life in which you and your partner feel boxed in, limited, or stressed. Without regard to any limits, start throwing ideas out that might help solve your problem. Insist that each of you come up with 10 to 15 ideas. Don't judge or criticize any of them. Keep encouraging each other to come up with more. Think your way out of that box. Write them down as fast as they flow.

ied to trust just one set of intellectual perspectives or to value just one way of thinking. You're both intelligent, and your relationship depends on two minds being better than one.

So what can you hope to accomplish by putting your heads together? In this chapter you'll practice using your minds together to solve problems, expand your horizons, or just have fun making sense with each other. It may not ever rank as high on your list of pleasurable activities, but making sense and making love can both be centers of joy in your relationship.

THE PROBLEM WITH PROBLEMS

You start at solving problems. Some philosophers view this as the primary function of the mind and tend to rate its effectiveness by the ability a person has to identify and solve the perplexing conundrums of life. A good, effective problem-solver is viewed as intelligent. Your marriage, of course, presents you with a nearly infinite array of opportunities to test your intelligence. Love means you're always solving problems.

If you have more bills than income, you have a problem that must be solved.

If your teenaged daughter refuses to respect her curfew, you have a problem.

If your son has a birthday party, and your boss has just informed you that attendance at the annual company conference scheduled for that very same weekend in San Francisco is mandatory, you have a problem.

The list could go on and on. You and your partner probably solve a dozen or more problems each day. Some tax your abilities to think creatively and to understand each other. Other problems you handle in a snap. Some linger for years, never really getting fully dealt with. This state of affairs can be frustrating but is very common in happy, long-term relationships.

The problem-solving challenge in your marriage is complicated by the fact that not every mind identifies or solves problems in the same way. In fact, wide variations exist in the way people think. You and your partner may have come to realize this about your own minds. You really don't think alike.

The problem with problems in marriage does not lie in the fact that they exist in incredibly large numbers. The problem with problems is that you and your partner never think the same way about solving them. You don't think alike, so you don't solve problems the same way. So if solving problems alone is tricky enough, solving them together presents a challenge of a different hue. It may sometimes frustrate you that the structure and movement of your life require that you embrace this challenge again and again. Love means you're always trying to solve problems that you and your partner think about in different ways.

A brief outline to keep your problem-solving process on task may be helpful. Many couples use a three-step process to start with and then build from there if the conversation gets complex. Try the following three-step path:

1. Clarify the problem by making sure you're both talking about the same thing. Define precisely what problem you're trying to solve.

2. Brainstorm the possibilities thoroughly. Allow each of you ample time to come up with ideas or possible solutions. Include the far-out ideas as well as the more conventional ones. Never use this time to evaluate or criticize an idea.

3. From the list of ideas you've created, select the one that seems to work best. Sometimes narrowing the list down to three or four helps make the selection go more smoothly.

Dominic and Natalie are moving through this process slowly. They have a clear idea of the problem: Aimee is staying out past her curfew, and they want that to stop. They're now presenting their ideas to each other. In this case, their ideas differ a great deal, but they're trying to be fair to each other and to re-spect the way the other thinks. How do you think their selection process will go?

PUZZLES

Mind talk is more than problem-solving. It also involves the simple but wonderful experience of intellectual connection and play. Not all mind talk is work; in fact, much of it is fun. You may discuss a book you've both been reading or a movie you've just seen. What do you think about it? The use of puns or intellectual word play in conversation also creates a sense of bonding and mutual understanding. For some couples, like Cindi and Jackson, this form of mind talk provides a significant part of their bonding and sense of intimacy.

Cindi is an administrative assistant in a healthcare company, and Jackson is struggling along as a freelance technical writer. Both are nearly obsessed with puzzles and particularly enjoy word games. One of their favorite activities is to litter their conversations with long strings of word play, puns, and word association. Most of their friends can stay with them for two or three exchanges, but after that, Cindi and Jackson are on their own. They try to limit themselves in public, but at times they elevate into flights of conversational word play and puns broken only by their peals of laughter and the occasional groan when an attempt falls flat or they violate one of their unwritten rules of engagement.

"Having Cindi and Jackson over for dinner," says one of their best friends, "is like speed-reading *Alice in Wonderland*. A lot is going on. I'm too slow to catch it all, but it's always fun to ride along."

Mind talk should be fun. It's a way of developing an awareness and appreciation of your partner's thought processes. It can be a lighthearted form of intimacy that revels in being smart in your own sweet ways. Which forms of mind talk bring you and your partner the most pleasure?

Going to a movie and discussing it later over coffee.

Reading a book together.

Debating recent decisions made by judges, politicians, or bosses.

Sharing perspectives on a recent magazine article.

Visiting a historical place and talking about its significance.

Working together on the daily crossword puzzle.

Being smart in your own way brings a sense of competence and security. Being smart together brings both of these and then adds pleasure.

POSSIBILITIES

Mind talk also enables you and your partner to expand your options. Ever had that feeling of being limited, controlled, or boxed in by some person or situation? It creeps into everyone's life from time to time. Allowing free thought to flow in relation to such situations can provide openings and opportunities previously missed.

Thinking outside the box or challenging each other to think in directions or dimensions you haven't visited before will allow your mind to free itself of patterns of thought that have you limited. Once free of these restrictions, ideas may spring into existence. As you allow these new perspectives to career around your head and bounce back and forth between you, new solutions or directions may present themselves. Your mind is far bigger than you give it credit for. Brainstorming allows you to find, appreciate, and apply some of its hidden gifts.

There are many tricks to use to help you brainstorm wildly and effectively. The process usually involves entering a change of perspective. You can do this.

Think in a different place.

Problem-Solving and Decision-Making

Solving a problem and making a decision are not the same. In this section, you're looking only at the way you think to solve a problem. You're using your mind. You may come up with solutions, but remember—a solution is not a decision, because it does not include the component of action. A solution is not a decision any more than the mind is the will.

You'll work with decisions in section five. For now, simply focus on thinking together, solving problems together, and being smart together.

Think while wearing a funny hat.

Think while standing where you usually sit, like on a chair or desk (like Robin Williams in the movie *Dead Poets Society*).

Think while sitting where you usually stand, like in front of the kitchen sink or in the shower.

Think standing on your head.

Climb a tree and think.

Think while looking out your attic window or from your rooftop (if it's safe).

To get your mind to think outside the box, you often must get your body outside its normal routines.

Jackson continually found himself pushed to think in this way. His occupation demanded that he constantly be seeking new outlets for his writing. He couldn't sit pat and let the world come to him. It didn't seem to know the way. So in order to make a living, he had to think outside the usual, outside the conventional, and outside the norms in order to sell his writing. Because his financial welfare was tied in with his decision, he talked with Cindi about the possibilities. In this case they were using mind talk to explore potential income opportunities, a different but necessary and enjoyable use of their minds.

Your conversations use mind talk then, when you need to solve a problem, share a thought, or expand your perspectives. In the next chapter you'll learn the simple guidelines that direct these conversations along the way so that by thinking together you can create an intimacy of mind.

eight

SEEK TO UNDERSTAND

In the previous chapter you encountered two couples. Dominic and Natalie think very differently, while Cindi and Jackson seem to have minds that flow along the same path. Does your relationship resemble one of these couples more than the other when it comes to mind talk?

In either case, mind talk has a certain structure that needs to be followed. Whether you think alike or differently, the guidelines in this chapter will help you talk to be clear and listen to comprehend.

The chapter ends with some thoughts about how to handle the emotions that rise up, like a fight at a hockey game, to trouble an otherwise smooth session of mind talk.

TALKING

In one sense, you hardly need instruction in mind talk. Your teachers in school have trained you for years in its use. Since kindergarten you've been told how to express your ideas in various ways: in speech, in writing, in class discussion. Whether trying to crack a difficult problem in math or entering your thoughts into a class discussion of world events, you've been using mind talk all your life. Your ideas have the best chance to be heard and understood by your partner when you follow your MIND: meet, inform, narrate, and deduce.

MEET

Remember when your first-grade teacher used to say, "Okay, class—now let's put on our thinking caps." That's a great way to invite a meeting of the minds. Set the stage for intelligent conversation with a clear invitation to your partner to think things through. This simple step will ensure that you and your partner will be set to meet mindfully.

Simple statements work best. "Can we put our heads together on this?" "Can we think about this together?" "I'd like to share my thoughts with you about something." These all work well. There's a great sentence in the Book of Isaiah in which the Lord graciously extends a mindful invitation to a wayward people: "Come now, let us reason together" (Isa. 1:18). That one is a little formal for most marriages, but something like it is worthwhile to put both of you into the thinking mode.

INFORM

Once you've agreed to meet, inform your partner of what you're thinking. As stated above, not all of us think the same way. This may lead to some confusion, but it's important to follow your own thought process as bravely, as clearly, and as thoroughly as you can. Your spouse will be struggling to stay with you, trying to understand how your mind is moving from point to point. Say it clearly, and follow the path that your mind naturally takes. Shed light on the subject. Illuminate your thoughts by stating the reasons you think as you do.

Now it must be said that your reasons may not make sense to anyone but you. You may think differently and in a different format than your partner does. For example, if you're gifted in music, your mind may not work with all the logic and precision of an engineer. Don't try to think like an engineer unless you are one. Explain yourself. Follow your reasoning. Try to let your partner know what you think and how you think. Both are important aspects of mind talk.

NARRATE

Never leave your thoughts in black and white—they deserve a little color. Once you've stated your opinion, jazz it up a little. After all, how convincing is a barebacked opinion? In addition to informing, then, you want to use illustrations, experiences, history, and examples to fill out your logic with splash and persuasion. Your thoughts deserve a rich and detailed embroidery. Add some colorful narration to your information.

For some this narration may look much like a logical syllogism; for others this enriching material may take more dramatic or colorful traits. You're attempting to convince your partner that you're right. Use all the material at your disposal, and deliver it with all the pizzazz you possess.

DEDUCE

The final step in a reasoned position involves stating your conclusion clearly and forcibly. Don't be shy about this. Trust your mind to think clearly and to arrive at trustworthy and significant deductions. Be firm and clear about what you think. There's joy in making sense in your own unique and valuable way.

You may expect your partner to follow the patterns for good mind talk listening and to be open to what you say. When the time comes for response and you reverse roles, you, too, will listen with an open mind.

LISTENING

A famous 15th-century prayer of Francis of Assisi contains the following words: "Grant that I not seek to be understood but to understand." This could be called the prayer of the mind talk listener. The vital position of the listener in mind talk can best be fulfilled as you seek to develop the determination and the skills to listen intelligently or to listen in order to comprehend. It may be helpful to think of the five steps in listening to mind talk as a BRANCH: believe, reason, ask, note, and challenge.

BELIEVE

In order to listen well in mind talk, you must believe in your partner's mind, and you must believe in the process of mind-meeting.

Belief in your partner's mind does not imply agreeing with every point. In fact, healthy couples often strongly disagree about many things. It's not agreement but intellectual respect that creates good mind talk. Your partner is bright and can use intellect to reach respectable, though sometimes debatable, conclusions. Failure to respect the mind of your partner will spell doom to all attempts to create intellectual intimacy.

The second part of belief involves your attitude toward the process of problem-solving. "Two heads are better than one"—this timeworn adage points to the fact that you and your partner, putting your minds together, can accomplish far more than either one of you can alone. Can you believe it?

REASON

Follow the train of thought, the expressions, the progression of reasoning, and the unique patterns of expression your partner likes to use. Like a hound dog keeping a nose on the trail, try to make the best sense of it you can.

In doing this, and with application of your mind, you'll learn the logic of your partner. What forms of intelligence does your partner excel in? How does that combination find expression? What keywords or ideas emerge? By asking these questions, you'll not only better understand the immediate thought your partner is attempting to share with you, but you'll also begin to perceive how that sometimes unpredictable mind moves from one place to another. As we said earlier, this movement is not the same for everyone, and learning your partner's thinking patterns will give you both a step up in facing challenging problems together.

Learning your partner's logic will involve learning the vocabulary that supports that thought. Words have meanings, but not everyone uses words according to these meanings. Personal logic often bends words into shapes and meanings that Webster never thought of. This is fine as long as you're following each other. Many couples have words that mean certain things to them that no one else is privy to.

Cindi and Jackson, the couple you met earlier, excelled in this skill. They even invented a few words to add additional color to their conversation and to enrich their ability to communicate certain thoughts to each other. In the flow of an intellectual conversation, knowing the words and how they mean what they mean will be helpful to avoid misunderstandings.

ASK

Good questions enrich and enliven conversation. The good listener always has a question to ask. Some questions help clarify the main ideas. Others help to push the mind to explore new areas or avenues of thought. As a listener, never be shy about questions; ask them often, ask them well. In mind talk you ask mindful questions:

What do you mean by that?

Can you be clearer about that?

Could you explain that more fully?

How do you see the connection between your two points?

Are there other reasons behind what you're saying?

A good listener can prevent useless tangents. A mindful conversation can go south in a hurry when a couple gets sidetracked on ideas, thoughts, and words that appear on the periphery of a good discussion but really have no claim to complete attention. A good listener weeds out these distractions and hones in on the main point, sometimes helping the talker stay on course.

NOTE WELL

As you're listening, be sure to pay careful attention to your own mind's reaction. If you find yourself strongly objecting to something, note what that is. If you find yourself being convinced by a particular argument your partner is making, take note of that also. Because mind talk builds itself on debate and interaction, you'll want to be able to clearly state your own mental process in response to what your partner is saying. Respect will prevent you from shortcutting the process through interruption or minimizing, but good mind talk depends on your ability to state clearly what you agree with and what you object to.

CHALLENGE

Mind talk makes sense only if both of you are thinking. After you've calmly and persistently tracked the logic of your partner, the time arrives for you to roil the waters of the conversation with some sturdy evaluation. A good listener does not simply accumulate information and opinions. In a more-or-less gentle way, seek to challenge the validity of the points your partner has presented.

The questions begin again, but this time they point not at your partner but inwardly toward your own mind.

Does this make sense to me?

Do these points really lead to that conclusion?

Has something been left out?

Do I see this problem in a different way?

Trying to honestly answer these questions will direct you to your own ideas and enable you to present a response to your partner that will enrich the discussion and lead to a more inclusive solution to whatever problem or idea you may be looking at. Take courage in this process, because your ideas may differ quite remarkably from those of your partner. Remember that agreement is not the goal of mind talk. Agreement may or may not follow this process of talking and listening. Your task as a listener revolves around understanding both your own and your partner's ideas. Understanding must always precede agreement. Therefore, seek to understand.

THOUGHTS AND FEELINGS

Talking with each other would be fairly simple if thinking conversations could be bottled up in one container and feeling conversations could be wrapped in another. But no such clear division exists in couple conversation. The matters that you wish to talk about reasonably may have some unreasonable strings attached to them.

You may think you're talking logically about saving money for a trip to Pennsylvania and suddenly realize that you're getting tense and terse with each other. You're getting upset. Is it anger? Frustration? Is it because you've not really talked about the fact that driving to Pennsylvania means you'll be driving right past your mother's house? How long will you stop there? Do you really want to stop at all? Are you worried that she and your spouse will argue once again if you stop? How did all these feelings and fears arise in the middle of a reasonable conversation?

These emotional ambushes happen to every couple. It's nothing to be ashamed of. The fact is, however, that when these strong feelings arise, they disrupt the conversation, and the two of you begin talking in different dimensions. The problem you wished to deal with is left frustratingly behind, and the futile attempts to communicate across dimensional lines lead to an ever-growing sense of loss and distance.

Talking about feelings and talking about thoughts are two very different conversations. They require different ways of talking, and they require different ways of listening. If you're getting emotional and your partner is staying logical, your conversation will not create understanding and probably won't end well. If the ability to talk mindfully evades you because of the strong feelings that are coming up, it's better to stop the conversation right then and there. You can no more solve a problem together when you are emotionally overcharged than you can when you are overtired, overextended, or overstressed. Don't even try.

If your feelings insistently and consistently disrupt your mind talk, it may be time to give those feelings your undivided attention. This involves a different style of conversation, soul talk. We'll explore soul talk in section four, but first we need to look at some of the many ways you and your partner think.

nine

PATHWAYS OF THE MIND

∾

Successful mind talk depends on your ability to understand how your partner thinks. The steps of thinking, however, vary a great deal from person to person. That's because while we're all smart, we're smart in different ways. Howard Gardner, professor of human development at Harvard University, in his book *Frames of Mind,* presents a way of understanding these different ways of thinking. Gardner names seven different ways to think, understand, and conceptualize. He calls these the seven intelligences, though he quickly points out that his list is only suggestive and that other intelligences probably exist.

As you consider the summaries of these intelligences, remember that both you and your partner have varying levels of strength in several of the approaches on the list. The list intends to enrich your understanding of each other and the unique ways you think and the equally unique ways you talk about your thoughts. As you begin to recognize your spouse's strong forms of intelligence, your appreciation and respect should grow also. You may well find yourselves in some of the following.

PATHWAY 1: LANGUAGE

Linguistic intelligence involves the use of words and of language. The fact that you enjoy talking with friends can be motivated by an inspiring speech or sermon, and the fact that you appreciate a good book demonstrates that you possess a high level of linguistic intelligence. You and your partner probably use words and language more than any other single medium to communicate your thoughts and feelings to each other. Linguistic intelligence, indeed, serves a foundational role in the relationship.

While this intelligence is to some degree shared by all, some have a particular gift in this area. Language and words for these gifted people are not seen as simple tools for communicating clearly. The words themselves have a fascination and a purpose all their own. Finding and using not just any word but rather the absolutely right word consumes their energy and fosters their delight. These people simply love words.

Those gifted in linguistic intelligence often become writers or poets. They feast on the use of language and revel in a well-turned phrase. But poet or not, you or your partner may have a strong gift in the use of words. The strongest mental tools the linguistic intelligence uses center on language, expression, and phrasing. Linguistic people often have an amazing memory for words and sentences they've heard. In analyzing and discussing problems, it's well to remember that linguistically intelligent people tend to see reality in term of words and sentences. Actions, experiences, and intentions may mean less and have less to do with a possible solution. The eloquent are not always grounded. They'll likely remember what you said much more accurately and much longer than what you did. If you're married to a person with high linguistic intelligence, be careful what you say.

PATHWAY 2: MUSIC

The second form of intelligence focuses on tones, pitches, rhythms, and melody. If this intelligence dominates your think-

Your Song

What's your favorite kind of music? Your partner's favorite? How does the presence of these musical styles affect your relationship?

Your sense of closeness?

The gaps between you?

How are you both seeking to understand and enjoy the musical preference of the other?

ing, it probably appeared very early in your life. In fact, we probably all learned the basics of music listening to our mother's voice while in the womb. The pleasure and response to music continues from early childhood on. Your musical intelligence shows itself in a number of ways. Sometimes a song heard on the radio on the way to work will stick in your head all day long. Or you'll find yourself humming a melody constantly, to the amusement (or annoyance) of those around you.

Musicians think in tonal and harmonic ways. Tied to these tones and the movement of music in their minds, they often express the moment's emotion, as music does. Powerful ideas and feelings can be evoked, shared, and communicated without ever seeing a need for the clumsy addition of words and sentences.

Even if most people have musical intelligence to some degree, those who possess it to a greater extent value its experience far more than others do. Music enters the mind to bring pleasure, a change of mood, or speak of the depth of human experience and emotion. For these people, music, tones, and patches of melody play continually in their minds. Consequently, the tones and melodic flow of a typical conversation can have meanings and significance that others may not be aware of.

If you or your spouse is strong in musical intelligence, you encounter the meaning of music everyday. A small, vocal inflection carries importance. A melody sings the world of experience.

PATHWAY 3: LOGIC

Logical-mathematical intelligence presents a third way of thinking. In a world of technology and computers, this form of intelligence has very high value. Logicians and mathematicians move from the physical world of objects very quickly to the mental world of abstractions. The movements of and relations between objects interest them far more than the objects themselves. If a beautiful bird flies into the vision of this type of thinker, the interest will tend to focus not on the beauty or grace of the bird but on the speed of flight, the proportion of wingspan to body length, and the weight in kilos of bugs this bird has eaten today.

Thought within this intelligence is clear, almost stark, and moves along closely defined lines. The mathematical formula, the logical syllogism, the chain of reasoning demonstrate the way any problem can be approached. A logical reason exists for everything that happens, and a logical solution exists for every problem posed. The clarity and confidence of the logical-mathematical intellect pose its strength but also mark the most frustrating element for a partner. Hamlet's friend expressed this frustration in the words "There are more things in heaven and earth, Horatio, than are dreamt of in your philosophy."

PATHWAY 4: SPACE

Spatial intelligence has to do with the ability to perceive and analyze the shape and movements of objects. You probably remember being tested for this intelligence. Pictures of rather complex objects were shown, and you were asked to rotate them in your mind and then identify which of several possibilities fit. You may have thoroughly enjoyed theses tests and had fun figuring them out. If so, your spatial intelligence is probably fairly high. If you hated these tests and had absolutely no clue which answers fit, you probably score low in this intelligence.

The ability to recognize forms, conceptualize how they would look from different perspectives, and even to conceptualize logistical and mathematical problems in spatial terms comprises the basics of spatial intelligence. Practically speaking, this means that you formulate, evaluate, and remember situations according to position and relative movement. Picasso, for example, is said to have remembered in close detail nearly every scene in his life. You, too, may remember a social gathering by recalling where each person sat, when and how movement occurred, and

Give Me Some Space

Have either of you ever had to say, "Give me some space"?

What were the circumstances?

What was the response?

What's the difference between physical and emotional space?

How do you handle space in your relationship?

What changes would you like to see?

how the room was set up. Your detailed memories of these spatial features may eclipse your sketchy and incomplete recollections of conversations, speeches, or background music.

People who excel in spatial intelligence make good engineers, architects, artists, carpenters, decorators, and builders. The use of these gifts has great value in society and relationship. This is partly due to the structure and beauty of objects that these gifted people either create or make us aware of. Another valuable contribution is their ability to view objects, movements, and people from differing perspectives. A person who has this ability can help others see familiar situations and people from perspectives that may add to appreciation and understanding.

In relationship, the emphasis on spatial relations can frustrate the problem-solving process. The following byte of conversation may sound familiar:

Sue: "I just need to know that you love me. I must feel that I'm number one in your life, that you're truly committed to this relationship and making it work."

John: "I'm here, aren't I?"

John's blunt statement seems like a refusal to enter the emotional and intentional aspects of the relationship. It seems far too simplistic and even evasive to constitute a serious response to Sue's plea. But what may look like an effective emotional blockade may be John's way of opening a door. To a strongly spatially oriented person, a declaration of physical presence may be the central statement of commitment and not just a prelude to relationship.

If you or your spouse appear to be particularly gifted in spatial intelligence, you may expect some communication difficulties. Dealing with a leaky roof may not present much tension, but dealing with your sassy adolescent daughter, a task that requires numerous intelligences, may be a much more difficult problem to solve together.

PATHWAY 5: MOVEMENT

Dancers, athletes, and instrumentalists exemplify those who have a particular gift in bodily-kinesthetic intelligence. This way of being smart involves two components: the ability to control the motions of your body and the capacity to manipulate objects such as piano keys, chisels, or a basketball with skill. This intelligence, as with all the others, usually works in combination with another. The pianist usually combines musical intelligence with bodily-kinesthetic intelligence to play a Beethoven sonata. A dancer must be proficient in the bodily aspects of movement as well as demonstrate an ability to interpret human emotion.

If you show an exceptional love for and skill in bodily motion, you show intelligence in this area. Taking things apart and putting them back together, like lamps, telephones, cars, and so on also indicates ability in bodily kinesthetic intelligence.

Sitting down to solve a problem when one of you tends to excel in this intelligence requires the ability to see things from the perspective of movement, action, dexterity, and physical manipulation. The leaky roof should present an agreeable challenge to the athlete, but the recalcitrant adolescent presents issues not easily solved physically. The opportunity to enjoy a physical activity together, however, may provide a gateway to the adolescent's mind.

Remember that talking, an activity that requires linguistic intelligence, may not necessarily be a strong point for the bodily intelligent person. Professional athletes, no matter how skilled and competent on the field of play, usually stumble about in the broadcast booth. The notable exceptions to this only prove the rule. Don't expect verbal eloquence from your bodily gifted partner. Try, rather, to understand the meaning of movement.

PATHWAY 6: SELF-AWARENESS

The final two intelligences are both personal. The first per-

Body-Mind Talk

Sharing physical activities can be a way of intelligent communication. How do you and your partner communicate while hiking? Walking? Biking? Playing a sport? Doing a project?

How do these activities help you understand each other better?

sonal intelligence directs itself inward. The capacity to know and to understand what lies within defines this way of knowing. What do you feel? What motivates you? What goes on in your heart? If the answers to these questions jump readily into your mind, you possess this form of intelligence. Surprisingly, the ability to answer these questions evades many people. To ask a question about feelings may send such a person into agonizing silence and shame.

This silence may point to some sort of denial or avoidance. At other times, or with other people, it may in fact be due to a less developed and refined inward personal intelligence. Sometimes a person says, "I don't know how I feel about that," and it really is that simple.

It's important to note that the capacity for being aware of your own internal processes of feelings, dreams, and motivations differs from the feelings themselves. Being angry, for example, is a different experience than reflecting on your anger once it's passed. Analysis of your angry feelings uses this inward sense of your personal intelligence. Analysis involves the mind. The ability to do this in a timely and constructive way is vital to your relationship and is the lynchpin of the listening skill of regulation that we discussed in the first chapter.

Proficiency in awareness and understanding of your inner dynamics points to inward personal intelligence, whether you center on dreams, emotions, or memories. You and your partner may not have an equal measure of this intelligence, but with care and exploration you can develop it. The following chapter will discuss the realities of these inner dynamics, called the soul, at greater depth.

PATHWAY 7: INSIGHT

One aspect of personal intelligence turns inward; the other aspect points in the opposite direction. Outward personal intel-

Morality

Talk together about the following poles of morality: Good vs. evil. Right vs. wrong. Leadership and Integrity. Justice and Injustice.

Does one of you show more passion or insight in these discussions? Are you both leaders in this sense, or does one of you have different intellectual gifts?

ligence focuses on the dynamics and motivation of others. The gift of this intelligence enables you to comprehend the "moods, temperaments, motivations, and intentions" of the individuals around you. People highly gifted in this domain make good politicians, leaders, parents, coaches, and counselors.

This form of intelligence often allows a person to look at issues as they pertain to an entire group. Moral issues, for example, can be seen plainly and clearly as what is good or not good for a society. Men and women with strong outward personal intelligence can offer leadership and guidance in places where others may be confused or lacking a moral compass. The value of direction must always be examined, however, as some of the most gifted men in outward personal intelligence have become the most evil despots in history. The intelligence of Hitler and Stalin enabled them to possess power to destroy while leaders such as Gandhi and Churchill used similar gifts in a markedly different manner.

To get back to the way this intelligence impacts your relationship, look at how well you and your spouse understand each other's deeper nature. What makes him tick? What's driving her? What does she really, really want? It's no crime if one of you answers with a perplexed "I haven't a clue." But such an answer signals that there's room for further development of this intelligence and plenty of space for the style of conversation discussed in an earlier chapter.

Each of these intelligences presents a pathway toward solving the problems you and your spouse face in your life together. Both of you have gifts in a number of these intelligences. As you think about them, talk about them, and use them, you'll continuously become more adept at solving problems together and go deeper in your knowledge of each other. You possess a unique combination of intelligences that's supplemented by the combination that you create as you bring your minds together. Learn to appreciate how very smart you are.

section four
SOUL TALK

The stretching of the soul is like the painful opening of the body in birth. It is so painful in the doing that we often will attempt to avoid it, even though such opening is ultimately full of pleasure and reward.
—Thomas Moore

Relationships fail not because we have stopped loving but because we first stopped imagining.
—James Hillman

ten

MY SOUL IS A LEAF

∞

Avery sips his iced tea and watches a bright green leaf flutter on its branch halfway between the blue sky and the dark earth. His words catch Michelle mid-swallow. "My soul is a leaf," he says with a slight grin, and she nearly chokes on her Diet Coke.

She has never heard Avery talk this way. She has no idea what brought on such thinking but would like to hear more. It feels like an opening. After a brief hesitation, she stretches out her one-word response the way people do to sound interested, inviting, and questioning all at the same time.

"Oook-kaaay?"

They sit in silence watching leaves.

Michelle finally decides to prime the pump a little, maybe get him restarted. "Your soul is a leaf—and?"

"Yeah," he says. "First it stretches out, seeking to embrace the light and air surrounding it, sensitive to every hint of breeze, opening to every ray of light, enduring every blast of storm. But then it also remains deeply connected, holding tightly to the tree, staying hooked to the branch, trunk, and roots. It refuses to let go. Its life depends on that connection."

Michelle's cell phone begins to play Beethoven's Ninth. "It's Mom," she says with only a slight rolling of her eyes. "I'll just be a minute." By the time the phone call ends, Avery has finished his tea, sealed up his contemplations, and started up the lawn mower. No more soul talk today. But Michelle is right. This conversation is an opening, and Avery and Michelle are beginning a journey they've both longed to take. They're becoming soul mates.

What is the soul? Avery has caught part of the answer in his reflection on leaves. The soul is that part within us that reflects a double movement. It stretches out in awe to receive light and order from what lies beyond. It seeks the infinite in the hand of nature and in the expanse of the starry sky. It searches for a sense of comfort and meaning in the stately repose of the mountain, the tickling joy of the brook, the passion of the wind. The soul seeks to explore and know these infinite realities.

At the same time, the soul plunges down into the depths of being. Deep historical and familial patterns draw its attention. Who am I? Why do I do the things I do and feel the ways I feel? What lies in the depths of that mysterious pool of my unconscious? Your soul not only stretches to the heights of heaven, but it also digs in to the roots of human experience.

A major challenge you face as a couple relates to how you talk about all this stretching and digging. At times your soul may be content to close in on itself and brood like a hen on eggs. You may feel somewhat hesitant or insecure about expressing your soulful experiences. At other times you may find your soul bursting out in the joyous cry of a rooster at dawn only to find your partner overwhelmed at the strength of your feelings. Intimacy of soul presents problems.

Not the least of these problems is defining just what a soul really is. Soul is so complex an idea that, like Avery and his leaf, we need metaphors to grasp it. Metaphors are very helpful because they form pictures to help us see more clearly. On the other hand, they're limited because they only illustrate certain aspects of the reality and can never show us the concept in its entirety.

What picture jumps into your mind when you say the word *soul?* One popular and persistent metaphor is that of a fluttering, ghostlike shape that lives inside you and leaves when you're dead. Ghosts have been a common and valuable image of the soul for centuries. This metaphor points to the idea that the soul lives past the body or that the body is enlivened—made alive—by the soul that lies within it.

Avery's metaphor of the leaf points to the way the soul stretches between two infinities, one inward and the other outward. It's a very good, if somewhat incomplete, metaphor. Other metaphors exist. What are some of yours?

Spiritual chemistry?

A journey?

An energy field?

A garden?

A secret room inside?

The wilderness?

Your metaphor for soul can be valuable in helping you and your partner begin to understand each other more deeply. Use these ideas to enrich your conversation. You'll probably develop a favorite picture for your soul, but always be open to the insight that other metaphors can give you.

This section focuses on conversations of the soul. After a look here in chapter 10 at what helps this aspect of yourself to flourish, chapter 11 offers some clear guidelines to enable you to consistently and confidently talk in this realm together. These guidelines will be followed by a consideration of four pathways to the soul: emotion, imagination, memory, and myth. The pathways help identify what to talk about when you share your soul.

To restore the soul of your marriage, first focus on the three intangibles your soul uses to provide health and meaning to your life: identity, growth, and relationship.

THE REAL YOU

Who are you? With leaves the answer is easy. The shape of a leaf tells the tale of its identity. Stoop and pick one up, and you can instantly tell where it comes from: an oak, maple, palm, or apple tree. Each one easily declares itself as part of a family.

Your soul, too, bears the marks of its identity. It carries a legacy that has been hewn and shaped for generations in your family. You have certain qualities, certain structures, a certain soul-shape that can be identified with a larger family or group. But you remain unique. Deep inside, you're remarkably different from even your closest relative. You may look a bit like Uncle Jim or walk like Aunt Geneva, but ultimately there can be no mistake. You are you. It's precisely this uniqueness, the real you, that you wish to communicate to your partner.

As you begin the process of sharing your soul, you may collide head-on into some surprises. Soul-sharing is not simple or predictable, because your soul is complex. This should come as no shock to you when you stop to consider the complexity and variety characteristic of your family, the ones who brought your soul to life. Your soul, like your family, has its strengths and weaknesses. It's locked in an unending attempt to balance its residing opposites: light and dark, masculine and feminine, open and secret, public and hidden away, knowing and not knowing.

Some of these struggles are up-front, obvious, and clearly accessible to you. Others may be locked deep within you, hidden, unspoken, and even undiscovered. As you share your soul with your partner, you'll probably start with the obvious and then go deeper and deeper as you gain confidence and skill. Some of what you may have to say will have been expressed to only a few very close friends and family members. Some of what you say will never have been spoken to anyone before.

The adventure of soul talk lies on this very path of mutual discovery and disclosure. It creates a mysterious sense of wholeness that comes from knowing deeply and of being deeply known. Because you'll be uncovering both the agony and ecstasy of what lies within, soul talk will be a long, winding path, a lifelong adventure.

Part of what makes soul talk so difficult is the vulnerability it brings to the conversation. You know that you're not perfect. Your soul carries ills, pains, and imperfections. Soul talk will reveal flaws and contradictions. You know that a close inspection will uncover matters that you may have wished to keep secret. How will your partner respond to your deep imperfections? Fear may bind these matters deep within, stashed away as if inside a locked chest in the basement. As you gain skill and confidence in soul talk, these chests can be opened, and that true and deep knowledge of what's inside can become part of your relationship.

SOUL GROWTH

Let's stay with Avery's metaphor a little longer. What can a leaf teach us about soul growth? The leaf starts as a small green bud, just a tiny splash of bright green against the darker bark of the branch. But that tiny splash of green holds promise, a promise fulfilled as summer comes and that bud gradually grows into the mature and colorful leaf. Later, as cooler weather creeps into the sky, this leaf, once totally green, begins to take on shades of brilliance never imagined possible. This wild color lasts for a time and then succumbs to the even colder wind and the natural rhythms of life. Soon it falls back to replenish the earth.

So also with your soul, each stage of development depends on the full expression and health of the preceding stage. Each step along the way has its own beauty and vulnerabilities. Through a similar series of expressions, the soul develops. You start young and clean, a splash and promise all your own. Slowly you grow and mature, becoming stronger and wiser as time goes by. In time you ripen into full color, offering the world your glory. Then, when the time is right, you'll move slowly along on your journey, your brilliant shades illuminating those who are close by and your gifts enriching others even after your time here is over.

Your soul's growth, so vital to a healthy, wholesome life and illustrated beautifully by the life of a leaf, can be maintained in many ways. As nature has provided an example of growth, so also it can be a continual source of development for your soul. Walking in the woods, along a trail in the park, or on the beach calms and develops your soul. Greeting the sun in the morning and watching the moon at night open you up to the infinite. The flowers you grow in your living room, the dog that accompanies you through the house, and the cat that plays with your ball of yarn all speak of the wonder of nature that envelops you. Your soul loves to tune itself to nature.

Soul development also lies at the heart of your faith and religious tradition. All spiritual paths have this theme in common. In particular, the spiritual disciplines of prayer, service, community life, and celebration fill your faith tradition and foster your growth and development. As you dedicate yourself to these disciplines, your soul expands, inviting God to visit and to change you.

Soulful pursuits are not limited to church and nature. Your soul absorbs nourishment from all aspects of its environment. The people you spend time with, the books you read, the movies you watch—all of these contribute to the growth of your soul. Art, writing, journaling, and singing are activities that feed your inner self. When done as an expression of inner grace, hobbies such as archery, golf, and quilting can nourish the soul.

No soul grows alone. Like the leaf, it enjoys ecstatic conversations with any number of significant partners. The breeze, the sweet moisture of fog, the gentle, delicious rain, the warm sun all contribute their fair share to what that leaf becomes. In the same way, nourish your soul with rich experiences and influences.

THE SOUL OF MARRIAGE

Your developing soul longs for deep companionship, a fellow traveler along the inner path. You seek a listening ear and an understanding heart. You thrive in relationship. This is why Michelle welcomed Avery's foray into the realm of soul. She wanted company there. She wanted a soul mate. The soul seeks for nothing as much as for the peace of a deep and unqualified acceptance. As your soul develops, you'll find a pressing need to express what's happening. You, like Michelle, listen for that "Yes" that validates and affirms your soul's struggles, dreams, memories, and contradictions.

Your first concern has been to find that peace with God. That relationship in which you find acceptance, forgiveness, and unconditional love provides, in Paul's words, the peace that "passeth all understanding" (Phil. 4:7, KJV). Augustine's famous prayer points to the same reality: "Our souls are restless until they find their rest in Thee."

This primary spiritual relationship can be joined by others who support your sense of peace and acceptance. Your pastor, your parents, your closest friend all may nurture your soul in one way or another. They may also be joined by a counselor, a spiritual guide, or a mentor. You may be blessed to enjoy one or more of these soul-builders. If so, you know the joy and relief they can provide. You have experienced the inner strength and guidance of their love.

Of all earthly and human relationships, marriage seems best designed to enrich your soul. As your most intimate and long-lasting relationship, it's perfectly aimed to go deep, to move smoothly through the joys of body and mind to create a truly satisfying relationship. What you provide each other by becoming soul mates is a secure foundation for your emotional and spiritual life.

Marriage grows the soul, but as with body and mind, this deep sharing requires conversation. Avery and Michelle, like many couples, had each experienced profound moments in their lives when their souls encountered God, a higher meaning, deepest love, profound grief and disappointment, and the mystery of life. But these experiences alone could not make them soul mates. They needed to talk about these rich experiences. You can't be soul mates without soul talk. The soul of marriage is deeply connected to soulful conversation. When Avery said, "My soul is like a leaf," he opened the soul's door.

Though talking about your soul and about matters of the soul is very important to your relationship, it's not always easy to express yourself deeply. There are fears and vulnerabilities that beset you when you try. But by talking about matters of the soul, soul talk, you'll lock yourselves powerfully and deeply to each other.

The next chapter will show you how to confidently enter the realm of the soul with each other in conversation: soul talk.

eleven

DEEPLY KNOWING, DEEPLY KNOWN

∾

Therese was a brick wall when it came to the furniture in her new living room. Her husband, Curt, a general building contractor, was peeved. He had assumed that once she had made her point, she would relent. He whisked her in to several furniture stores. She played along with the shopping part, seemed to have fun talking about what might look good, but then at crunch time she adamantly refused to buy a thing. Over the months her refusal to furnish the living room had whittled itself down to the three words she said over and over again: "Nothing more—until . . ."

Her parents and sisters were embarrassed when they had to bring their own chairs to a birthday party for Therese and Curt's seven-year-old daughter, Katie.

"Should we bring our own forks too?" scoffed Annie, Therese's oldest sister.

But Therese remained firm. She had not been fussy about the plans for the house Curt was building for their growing family. She asked for just one thing: a large living room with a fireplace. Now, with the house completed and the family moved in, Teresa absolutely refused to furnish the living room. At first it appeared to be a simple matter of indecision over what to buy. But as time went on, it was clear to everyone that something more was going on with Therese.

One day she angled two folding chairs in front of the fireplace, looked Curt squarely in the eye, and made her announcement: "We'll put nothing more in this living room until you and I begin to talk."

Curt tried to convince her. "I talk. I talk all the time."

But that plane wasn't going to fly with Therese. "I don't want that kind of talk. I want to talk like we used to when we were camping and sat out at night, under the stars and in front of the fire. Now, with your business, your fishing trips, your ball games, and your pickup truck, it's like you've forgotten how."

Therese and Curt have a soul talk problem common to many relationships. Talking deeply comes quite naturally in the flush of first love. The excitement of discovery and the warm seduction of romance can bring this kind of sharing out of a stone. How often, as new love wraps its arms around a couple, have you heard them say, "Talking comes so naturally with us. I'm saying things I've never told anyone before. I can't believe it."

But as time goes by, the pressures of daily life mount, and the newness of love settles into the routines of marriage. Deep conversation begins to get crowded to the side. Soon it can feel exactly as Therese said: "It's like you've forgotten how."

The loss of soul talk creates a hollow marriage. If losing light talk leads to chaos, and losing mind talk brings misunderstanding, then the loss of soul talk leads to loneliness. To feel lonely in marriage is a curse no one should have to endure, but reestablishing soul talk is not an easy task. If you attempt to open your soul and your partner is not attentive and affirming, you'll feel an even greater sense of rejection.

That's what makes soul talk risky. When you open up to

share your feelings, dreams, memories, or beliefs, you make yourself vulnerable. Expressing your deepest dreams and feelings carries uneasiness, a fear of being misunderstood or rejected. Rejection at this level is nearly intolerable. Even something as slight as momentary disinterest from your partner can carry a sting of pain. Outright criticism or rejection can send you over the edge. This happens because your walls are down, your disguises removed, exposing your true self.

In this way, soul talk differs from other forms of communication. For example, if your partner rejects an idea you have, you can handle it. Disagreement is part of mind talk. In the same way, if your partner resists your attempts to influence or change something that bothers you, that's fine. You expect resistance. You never intended to love a wimp who bends and conforms to your every wish.

But soul talk is different. If you open your soul, you need your spouse to be attentive, accepting, and acknowledging, or you'll be disappointed and hurt. Therese experienced that hurt every time she tried to open up and Curt brushed her off and hurried to his next task. She decided to press the issue and tried to use the magic of the fireside to rekindle their relationship. It was a valiant effort, but she found that even when Curt did sit with her by the fireplace, the conversation bumped and clanged along like an antique fire engine.

Therese and Curt were attempting soul talk but were unsure about the methods that lie beneath that style of conversation. Talking and listening in soul talk require certain skills.

TALKING

Because this style of conversation has such potential to wound, you must be very careful in approaching it. As the one sharing your soul, you'll be placing unusually high expectations on your partner, the listener in this context. It's vitally important for you to take responsibility to minimize the chances that misunderstandings occur. This requires energy and agreement. The acronym SOUL may help you when you're ready to express yourself deeply. Be sure to seek permission, open up, understand, and love.

SEEK PERMISSION

The cardinal rule in soul talk requires that only one person speak. This rule marks soul talk as unique among the styles of conversation as the others accept and even expect a great amount of back-and-forth, of statement and response, of point and counterpoint. Only in soul talk does one ask the listener to set aside personal responses and ideas and instead focus entirely on the message and feelings of the speaker.

Such a request places great demands on the listener, so you need to be clear and respectful when asking for this kind of listening ear. To listen to you disclose the deeper regions of your soul can be taxing. Your spouse may feel able to do it one day but not really be up to it the next. The amount of concentration and emotion that soul talk requires from the listener prevents the task from being taken lightly. Whenever possible, seek your partner's permission before entering this sacred space. Just a simple sentence can introduce the conversation and allow each of you to be clear that you're entering this personal area.

Of course, emotions are not always predicable. They flitter and fly whenever and wherever they choose, always on paths of their own. The same holds true for the other categories of the soul. So it's not always possible to corral this deeper part of yourself and save its expression for a certain time of day or a certain place. But if you practice being clear about these conversations when you're able, you'll increase your skill as a couple to recognize and respond appropriately to spontaneous revelations of the soul.

OPEN UP

When you're expressing matters of your soul, too much thought can get in the way. As risky as it may feel, it's best to let yourself talk without care or caution. Let the impressions, memories, and images flow freely. They may tumble over one another in a somewhat confusing fashion. At other times they may come slowly, with pauses and hesitant speech.

If you're an unpracticed pilgrim, you may stutter and stammer your way through your first soulful disclosures like a shy teen in speech class. Even your partner's encouraging smile and understanding words may not help you. That's okay. Take courage. Plunge in anyway. Open up even when you feel hesitant to do so.

Soul talk does not deal with contrived solutions with logical constructs or with either grammatical or narrative precision. Soul talk runs like a mountain stream: dancing over rocks, singing over little waterfalls, settling for a moment in a deep pool of reflection, only to go rushing on again in search of the next adventure. If you truly want your partner to know you deeply, sweep away the dam and let the river flow.

UNDERSTAND

Soul travelers need persistence. While soul talk may sometimes resemble a cascading mountain stream, at other times it may feel more like digging a well. Your soul lies deep within you, and many layers of habit and repression may need to be removed in your attempt to understand it. Your courage and determination to get to the bottom of your feelings, coupled with your partner's willingness to help you explore them, can make this journey into yourself successful and eminently rewarding.

The vulnerabilities of disclosure make it all too easy to lock away the emotions and memories of a lifetime. You may get stuck in the unearthing process. If this happens, try a different way of expressing yourself to get things going again. Just as there are many aspects of the soul, there are many ways to communicate its life and energy. Sitting down together at the fireplace and looking deeply into one another's eyes is certainly one way. There are many more. Try writing notes or even love letters to each other. Poetry has been called the wings of the soul. When was the last time you wrote a poem to your lover? Music provides another instrument of the soul. A well-played melody can speak volumes. Despite the degradation and abuse the guitar has been forced to endure in these times, a love song sung to the soft strumming of a few chords remains among the most gripping and beautiful examples of soul talk.

If expressing feelings proves difficult to you, start somewhere else. Talk about your memories. Or share your hopes and dreams. What would you do if you came into a lot of money? Why? Be creative in your soul talk. Your creativity is a vital connection of your soul. When you let that light shine, you not only experience the joy of self-expression, but you also allow your partner to experience the wonder of what lies within you. Creativity is the midwife of soul mating.

LOVE

Demonstrate your love by attending to the needs of your listener just as your listener is paying attention to you. Remember that in all this digging down and opening up, you have a partner who cares enough to listen, explore, and affirm what you reveal. Listening can sometimes be a very difficult task, and your sensitivity to its difficulty will greatly help your partner.

Matters of the soul can overwhelm both speaker and listener. Your listening partner must always have the option to call time out and let things settle down a bit before moving on. Breaks may be necessary due to the amount or confusion of material. They also can be needed if the soul talk is delving into sensitive or difficult areas.

Also keep in mind that soul talk offers the talker a vast array of temptations for misuse and subtle jabs. Your listener is vulnerable, because, as explained in the following section, the steps of listening to soul talk involve letting go of counterpoints and reactions in order to focus on acceptance. This vulnerability must always be treated with respect by the talker. Subtle or not-so-subtle attempts to criticize, blame, accuse, or manipulate the listener definitely fall outside the pale of healthy and loving soul talk.

LISTENING

A story in Exod. 3:1-5 relates how Moses, while walking through the wilderness, caught sight of a bush that appeared to be on fire yet was not burning up. As he turned aside to focus attention to this strange blaze, he heard a strong voice say, "Take off your shoes, Moses. You are standing on holy ground" (author's paraphrase).

It might be good for all of us to remember these words when we're engaged in soul talk. To be given permission to enter another person's soul is indeed a holy exchange. Listening requires respect, even a sense of awe.

Your responses, then, are most helpful if they're softly questioning, exploring, and affirming. Don't try to change what you hear. Don't attempt to take the feelings away, minimize the memories, or limit the imagination. Accept them. Honor them. Respect them. You're standing on holy ground. The listener's role in soul talk, then, asks that you follow the acronym LEAF: let go, explore, affirm, and finish.

LET GO

Soul talk involves placing your partner on the center stage of your conversation and focusing completely on what's being said. Let go of your reactions, your pains, your concerns, your ego, your sudden impulses. Say to yourself, *I'm on sacred ground here, and I must be totally respectful to what I am hearing. The soul of my partner is worthy of my complete attention.*

Letting go may mean taking a huge cleansing breath or two. It may require a silent prayer for peace. It may mean engaging in a clearing activity like exercise or a walk. Such strategies help with soul talk, because the listening task is so focused and intense. You may need to break occasionally during your partner's soul sharing to regain this cleared, listening position.

Having cleaned out your own baggage for a few minutes, focus everything on the words and message of your spouse. The primary way for this to happen is to sit quietly and to look steadily at the speaker. Your eyes send the clearest message about your bent of attention, and your partner will assume that you're paying attention to whatever you're looking at. Eye contact complements soul talk.

Be alert for soul appearances. Your partner may slip into soul talk at any time and without prior notice. Soul talk presents unique challenges, because it does not appear in predictable ways. The soul seethes, bubbles, or ripens and cannot be confined to any timetable. Emotions dart in and out of your partner's awareness like rabbits in a glade. Aromas, melodies, or even a gentle breeze can trigger memories that have lain dormant for years. Sometimes these inner events make their way into speech at odd or inconvenient times.

While a talker is asked to seek permission, no one can remember to do that every time. In fact, sometimes that will seem very awkward and break the spontaneity of the moment. If you carry in your mind the four categories of soul—emotions, imagination, memory, and myth—you'll recognize the moment it appears in your spouse's speech. Upon identifying the signs of soul talk, you can shift your listening posture from mind talk or light talk to the concentration and care that soul talk listening demands. Becoming adept at soul recognition will save innumerable problems and frustrations for you and your partner.

EXPLORE

The task of the soul-talk listener involves exploration, not explanation, prediction, analysis, or any of the other temptations of the mind. You listen simply in order to find. "Explore" comes from the Latin verb meaning to search out. Like Columbus, Magellan, and Lewis and Clark, you want to find out what's there.

When listening to soul talk, use open, inviting questions. There are times when the soul talk just seems to flow like a river. At other times, because the content is distant or difficult to express, the talker may stumble, turn away, or grow strangely quiet. The listener wants to respectfully and gently help the words to flow again. The slightest hint of judgment or impatience may make things worse, but good, clear, open questions can open things up again.

Michelle's elongated and inquisitive "Ooook-kaaay?" urged Avery on when he started to open up. When that tactic failed, she turned to a questioning repetition of his words. "Your soul is a leaf—and?" Soul questions constantly seek to invite openness. They never seek specific answers. Had Avery remained quiet, Michelle might have tried other questions.

"Could you say more about that?"

"Yes, and then what?"

"Hmmm. That's interesting. Could you give me more?"

Practice asking these questions. And no less important, remember to wait patiently for the answers.

AFFIRM

When you're partner begins to talk from the soul, you may hear things you didn't know existed. You may hear shocking words, beautiful words, sad words, or ecstatic words. You may hear ideas, see pictures, relive experiences, or encounter a strength and resiliency you had hardly dreamed of. Whatever you hear, even if it surprises or pains you, always accept.

To fulfill the role of listener in soul talk requires a readiness or determination to be favorably disposed to what you hear. If you find that favorable posture slipping away from you, you must ask for a break. Without acceptance, soul talk leads to pain and distance. Expressing your soul lays bare the deepest, most secret part of yourself, creating vulnerability. If your listener rejects what you say, appears to lose interest, or grabs the focus back away from the message, it bothers. It feels as though your partner suddenly says, "You know, I don't really care about who you are after all." And that hurts.

Perception and habits may confuse a clear message of acceptance. Affirming your partner has less to do with what you say and more to do with how your partner hears you. Each of you must learn what communicates acceptance in the throes of vulnerability. For example, to one of you a hug may say in effect, "I've heard what you've said, and I accept it all as part of who you are." The other may find a hug patronizing or simplistic, a way of dodging the truth. Learning to accept and affirm each other forms the bedrock of soul talk.

The soul talk listener never, ever, ever says "but." Some of the most engaging, profound, and potentially productive ventures into the soul have been aborted by the sudden appearance of this word in the listener's response. To the speaker, it almost always sounds like resistance, second-guessing, and ultimately rejection.

This does not mean that you must always like what you hear. Soul talk can run the gamut from carefree exuberance to dark horror. Affirmation extends to each end of the soul's spectrum. It does not necessarily mean that you'll encourage your partner to act on the things that have been shared. But if they're seen as true and legitimate expressions of the inner being of that person you love, then you must accept and affirm them as part of who that person is right now.

FINISH

Soul talk begs for a clear end. To speak from the depths of feelings and dreams, to imaginatively walk along the roads of memory, or to explore the deepest beliefs and assumptions of life all expose a speaker in ways uncommon to an ordinary day. Talking about such things may leave you both vulnerable and exhausted. A good step in listening involves making an end of the conversation so both of you can safely leave the intensity of that moment and return to your busy life.

Abruptly moving or withdrawing from the conversation may leave the one speaking feeling abandoned and dismissed. Taking a moment to finish the conversation helps prevent the pain of such misunderstandings.

"Thank you for sharing yourself like that."

"Is there anything more you would like me to know?"

"What would you like from me right now? A hug? Some space?"

"It sounds as though you have more to say about this. Can we come back to it another time?"

Such questions and statements signal to you both that you're moving from soul talk into a different space.

"If I start expressing my feelings, I'll never stop." Some form of this fear plagues many couples. This assumption revolves around the idea that feelings act like some fountain or geyser. Once this hidden source of energy is tapped, everything held there will burst forth uncontrollably and continually.

While emotions sometimes result in this behavior, usually these fears are unfounded. Think of the soul more as a deep pool rather than a bursting fountain. You have control over the amount of time you spend in the cool waters of this pool, and you decide how deep you wish to dive. Couples who fear the fountain effect can often allay their fears by putting a hard time limit on their soul talk. Practicing with a time limit quickly gives a couple a sense of confidence.

twelve

PATHWAYS TO THE SOUL

ॐ

A quiet Tuesday evening finds Curt in his favorite chair, glancing through a magazine while waiting for the Red Sox game to start. Therese sets her book aside with a sigh and watches him flip the pages.

She finally speaks. "Curt?"

He recognizes the tone and stops flipping.

"Why won't you talk to me?"

He's just a little defensive. "What? We talk every day. I'm always talking to you. I call you on the phone to let you know where I'll be and when I'll be home. I talk with you during dinner. Hey—I'm talking with you right now."

"You talk with me, yes, but not about anything important—not about your feelings. I have to guess constantly about what's going on inside you. I don't know how you feel about anything."

Curt throws his arms out in a dramatic gesture. "What's there to know?"

Therese's eyes fill, and she fights to keep them from overflowing in the silence that follows. After a tense pause, Curt continues in a softer tone.

"You always seem to want these deep conversations. I'm just not a deep guy. I try sometimes. You know I do. But when we sit down for a fireside chat and you start digging around, you get mad and disgusted if I don't say the exact right thing. You seem to want me to say certain things, and I just don't know what they are."

"It's not about saying certain things, Curt. It's *anything*— anything that will tell me you're alive inside, that you feel something. I want you to stop running from me, stop hiding from me, and open yourself up. I want to know that I'm important enough to you that you want to share these things."

"I wish I had an answer. You know that you mean everything to me. All I can say to you is what I've said a thousand times. You tell me you want to know what's inside me. I look inside, and there's nothing there. I don't have the part you're looking for."

Therese stares at him a few moments without speaking. When she finally opens her mouth to respond, she notices his nervous glance at his watch and at the television set remote control that beckons from the table beside him. She murmurs a curse for the ball game, and when he doesn't respond, she picks up her book and leaves the room. Curt sadly stares after her. Then, with a sigh, he reaches for the remote.

Therese knows there's more to Curt than he'll admit. She knows he has feelings, hopes, and dreams. She's heard him relate memories that run deep in his soul. She watches him live a life of firm convictions and standards. And she senses that he struggles with what lies within. Those struggles keep them apart, however, because he seems unable to express these things to her. It's not that Curt doesn't have a soul. He just doesn't have access to it.

All couples need some clear and dependable directions to help them move to a refreshing expression and clear understanding of what lies within. You may be at a loss if someone

Love Letters

Write a love letter to your partner, and read it aloud just as you're going to bed. Or write a poem and read it while you're sharing a romantic dinner. Sharing your emotions through writing gives you the chance to be open, creative, and thoughtful.

says, "Tell me what is in your soul." But you have memories. You have hopes and dreams. Your life was shaped by certain beliefs and convictions. You certainly know frustration, excitement, fear, worry, and happiness. In talking about any of these, you travel down a pathway to the soul. After several trips, this pathway becomes familiar. Consistently using these pathways, you and your spouse can actually become what you may only have dreamed about: soul mates.

PATHWAY 1: EMOTION

Most of what you know about emotion comes from experience, not analysis. While intricate and highly technical definitions of emotion exist, your personal take on your feelings and experiences probably will capture more clearly to you and your partner what your emotions mean. That's because emotion has to do with the deeper, unique, and sometimes mysterious you.

For this reason, a look into the emotions of the person you love will usually open up viewpoints and perspectives you hadn't seen before. In sharing emotion, you plummet beneath the surface of your relationship and open up your truer, deeper selves. You've done it before. As a long and complicated rational discussion begins to wind down, you look your partner in the eye and say, "Okay. I understand all that. Now tell me how you *feel* about it."

This probing for emotion reflects your desire to know on a different level. But when you try, problems may appear. You may have been taught not to open this gateway. Your partner may find it difficult to know exactly how to communicate in this volatile sphere. Perhaps a look at some of the primary characteristics and functions of emotions will be helpful.

First, emotions fly away quickly. This fact may help quell the commonly held fear that once bogged down in the quagmire of feelings, it may take hours or even days to emerge.

Though the duration of certain emotions may vary, most appear only to pass away rather quickly. Even strong emotions like anger, happiness, fear, or excitement usually fill the awareness for only moments before they move past into other things.

This fact may seem to fly in the face of some of your experience. You and your partner may sometimes fight for days at a time. But consider the energy and planning it takes to extend the lifespan of any emotion for more than a few minutes. To be angry for three days requires an immense effort involving reminding yourself constantly of the offense, planning other angry things to say, and a determination to keep hanging on to the memory of the offense in spite of the temptation to let it go. By the same token, to feel loving and romantic for an entire evening will often demand the planning and execution of an elaborate series of events, activities, and behaviors. The same is true of other feelings.

Second, emotions are neutral. An emotion never carries morality on its shoulders. It can never be called good or bad. Neither you nor your partner can be called good or bad simply because you experience this or that emotion. Feelings come from an automatic response to what's happening or what you perceive to be happening around you.

In this respect, emotions resemble the reflex action of your lower leg when the doctor taps your knee with that little hammer. Your leg kicks out involuntarily, and the good doctor knows to stay clear of the path of your foot. In no way does that kicking action make you good or bad. It pronounces you normal. In the same way, when something good happens to you, you feel happy. When something bad happens, you feel sad or perhaps angry. Having these feelings demonstrates that you're healthy and normal, not good or bad. In this sense, emotions are amoral.

Third, all emotions have a purpose. Emotion provides both the direction and the motivation for change. When a feeling

How Does It Feel?

Together choose an emotion from the following list. Talk about a time when you've felt that way. Describe the context, your physical response—sweaty hands, red neck, butterflies in your stomach, and so on. How long did the feeling last? How was it finally resolved?

Happy	Bored	Giddy
Romantic	Sad	Angry
Restless	Excited	Discouraged
Silly	Anxious	Enraged
Ecstatic	Frustrated	Afraid
Nervous	Lonesome	Content
Hostile	Loving	

Your Wild Imagination

Complete the following sentence by filling in the blank. "In my wildest dreams, and without any restraints at all, I would see this happening in our _____."

Vacation	Sex life
Weekends	Next five years
Friendships	Next ten years
Use of money	Life mission
Church involvement	Family relationships

wells up inside of you, it's telling you something profound about yourself and the situation you're in. For example, fear, frustration, or anger signal danger and the need to change. These emotions tell you, "Do something." These responses may be accompanied by powerful physical urges to ensure that something does happen. These urges are sometimes labeled the "fight or flight" response and are marked by the tensing of muscles, adrenaline rush, or jitteriness. Functionally, these emotions are designed to be sure that you keep your environment and relationships safe and healthy.

In the same way, happiness, love, or contentment may include the physical responses of warmth, relaxed muscles, and the urge to stay close to what causes these feelings.

Fourth, emotions require expression. A passionate and hearty expression of your feelings allows your partner to hear what's going on inside you. The force with which you speak often moves in inverse proportion to your partner's ability or willingness to listen to what you say. The sharper the listening, the less intense the expression needs to be. If the listening smacks of dullness or drifting, you may need to be louder or more intense. Couples who yell at each other a lot often end up telling a therapist that they need to learn to express their emotions. Often the problem involves not the expressing but rather the listening to emotion.

Once the expression has occurred, the time comes for discussion. Sitting back and talking about the feelings you have helps to broaden and deepen your relationship. Discussion helps to point to better understanding and clearer expression and also helps create a mutual sense of direction.

Finally, feelings build self-knowledge. Knowing yourself emotionally means that you've tapped that deep reservoir of information about what moves you, what's important to you, what you care about, and what frightens you. Who do you love? What perks your interest? What makes you anxious? Tracking your emotions can help answer these questions. No one has access to this knowledge but you. Others, including your spouse, can only assume answers based on what you say and do.

In order to develop good soul talk, you may need to practice verbalizing your feelings. Check out the sidebar for a list of emotions and practice expressing these feelings with each other using good soul talk guidelines.

PATHWAY 2: IMAGINATION

The second pathway of the soul is imagination. Imagination has to do with the soul's ability to form images, ideas, and stories that don't spring directly from reality. Your soul is free to construct or concoct images and fantasies in any way it chooses. Reality does not regulate it. In fact, it's the difference and distance from reality that marks imagination for what it is.

Imagination is often associated with the words "fancy," "fantasy," "dream," "originality," "creativity," "invention," "inspiration," "verve," and "empathy." These words burst with life: a new idea, a new perspective, or a new way of doing things. Your imagination may be triggered by the experience of reality, but it's never bound by it. The soul strikes out to find paths and answers of its own.

In this way, dreams are tied to imagination. As a source of imagination, both common ideas of dreams fit this category. First, the dreams you have while sleeping are a movement of your soul. They have been understood in various ways: a message from God, the expression of the deep subconscious, the manifestation of the collective unconscious, and even the twist of a dyspeptic midnight snack.

In the context of your relationship, you need not solve the psychological or theological questions about what dreams are. But their significance makes it important to share your dreams with your partner. Tell your dreams. You may or may not come

Myths of Life

Consider the following belief statements. Talk about how you react to them on a gut level. Which ones turn you away? Which ones feel positive to you? Are there any that you live by?

Children should be seen and not heard.

Love conquers all.

Everything happens for a reason.

God is love.

My family comes first.

Time is money.

to an understanding of them. Laugh together about them. Take a stab at interpretation. Allow these significant night visitors to take their place in your relationship. Invite them in, and allow them to do their mysterious work.

The second meaning of dreams, as in daydreams, is also very important to the soul. Daydreaming happens when you're awake, creating images in your mind by allowing your imagination free rein in association, suggestion, and inventiveness. Sometimes these dreams may be quite fantastic with little connection with what is or possibly could be. At other times you may be creating images that can in fact become real if things go according to plan or wish.

Use imagination to enrich your life together. Sometimes it's helpful to pinpoint certain aspects of your relationship and let your imaginations run wild about them. For example, what can you envision your life together to be in five years? How about ten? If you allow your imagination free play in your sex life, what would that be like? If you were doing for work exactly what you would love to do, what would it be? How would it be different than today?

Soul talk helps turn dreams into words. You're trying to learn how better to communicate the depth and breadth of your imagination to your partner. Not every dream will come true, but rich dreams always enrich reality. A fish lays one million eggs in hopes that just a few will survive.

PATHWAY 3: MEMORY

You and your partner both have experiences locked away in places no one else has access to: your memories. Many of these memories have seldom or perhaps never been told. Some memories resemble quick mental snapshots, while others play full-length movies of things you've seen or experienced. These images help determine how you think and what you value. How familiar are you with the cache of memories that your spouse carries around?

The soul often moves along the lines of memory. Good memories can be fun. Part of building a lasting love lies in creating good memories together. The stories that surround the events of your life are vitally important and deserve to be told and retold. Remember the way you met? Was it by chance, the way Avery and Michelle met at the coffee shop? Or did someone set you up? What were some of the crazy things that happened on your wedding day? What was your best vacation? The craziest place you ever made love? Your best anniversary surprise?

Not all memories are good. Bad memories also have a place in your soul. Like bad dreams, they refuse to be ignored. Sharing these memories can be stressful and heartbreaking for both of you. Yet often, once shared and processed, these memories can be stripped of their power to hurt. Bad memories lovingly discussed can be healing for the soul.

Also consider those mysterious memories. These clips of trivial little events or comments don't seem to have much importance, but for some unknown reason they stick with you. Why? Have you explored this little collection together? The unknown person who visited the house one day, the scene in the country somewhere that you remember distinctly but can't place where it was, the look of blame from a teacher, the sound of a door slamming shut—these tiny scenes can clutter your memory with unanswered questions and surprising reactions. What would it be like to explore these things with your partner?

These memories, good, bad, and indifferent, are stored away in your souls and can be an almost infinite source of sharing, bonding, and conversation. Dig into this mine with energy and persistence. You're digging gold.

I Believe

Complete this statement five times each: "I believe_____."

∾

PATHWAY 4: MYTH

Myth defines another aspect of your soul. To some, myth means something that's untrue, not factual. But myth can be either fact or fiction. That's not the point. A myth, says the *American Heritage Dictionary*, is "any real or fictional story, recurring theme, or character type that appeals to the consciousness of a people by embodying its cultural ideals or giving expressions to deep, commonly felt emotions." That is, myth relates to the underlying beliefs, principles, and values that guide our lives. Your deeply held convictions carry you through rough times, bring focus to your endeavors, help to orient your experience in a broader context, and create meaning and direction in your life. Myth provides the beacon that helps you make choices about the way you live, what you live for, and how you evaluate your life and work.

Myth often takes the form of magnificent stories dealing with the mysteries and profundities of life. Some of these stories define an entire culture and present certain themes: the hero, conquest, love, the meaning of life, the significance of gender, the experience of the transcendent, death. The literature, stories, and poetry of a culture carry these themes in a contemporary style. Movies have become a dominant mythic expression in our culture. Some collections, such as the John Wayne movies or the *Star Wars* trilogy, have been powerful shaping agents in our culture.

The teachings and tenants of your religious faith carry these themes forward in a more traditional way. The stories in the Bible, while factual in nature, point us toward meaning and direct us on how to live our lives. For example, we love the story of David and Goliath not only because God gave David strength and courage to face the giant but also because when we face our own Goliaths, we need to have the faith and strength of David in our souls.

But not all myth is grand and epic in nature. Myth can also take the form of a small statement, adage, or capsule. These short statements summarize a way of thinking or a way of experiencing the world or the events that happen around us. For example, many interpret perplexing or difficult events with the belief that "everything happens for a reason." This simple statement enables a person to bring reason and order to what's experienced as a random and even harmful event. Most of us keep a few of these time-honored statements in our mind's pocket for quick reference.

Knowing each other deeply comes with recognizing, accepting, and exploring these statements and stories. While some are short and brief on the surface, they represent an entire process of thought and belief beneath the surface. Take time to unpack some of your favorites with each other.

Other values and beliefs cannot be summed up in a quick line. A person's religious faith, for example, is generally more complex and may require lengthy conversations to understand. The influence of early experiences in a church, the place of a respected pastor or mentor, gatherings and traditions at holiday seasons, the experience of prayer, the guidance and inspiration of Scripture or sacred writings—these and other aspects of religious life refuse to be squished into a sentence. Talking about them at length with your partner not only can deepen your faith itself but also can greatly enrich your soul connection with each other.

Another aspect of myth centers on ritual. Every relationship uses regularly practiced actions to embody shared beliefs and values. Rituals touch the deep meanings and currents of life. In marriage, for example, the ritual of sex enacts again and again the covenant and promises made in the wedding ceremony. And that ceremony itself is a ritual enacting the commitment made in the depths of the soul and in the broader circles of family and community.

In the same way, the countless rituals of life together point to the deeper commitments and experiences of the bond between you. Eating together, the morning kiss, listening to "our song," vacation at camp, birthday celebrations, and anniversaries—the list goes on and on. Rituals communicate the soul. The couple with strong, healthy rituals tends to be strong and healthy in other aspects of their relationship, because in these rituals they're continually bringing into the intimate present the host of commitments, feelings, experiences, and desires that form the soul of their relationship.

Pathways of the soul therefore include these four: emotion, imagination, memory, and myth. To become stronger soul mates, walk these pathways often with each other.

section five
HEART TALK

Listen and attend with the ear of your heart.
—St. Benedict

The education of the will is the object of our existence.
—Ralph Waldo Emerson

thirteen

RAIN FORESTS
AND DIRTY SOCKS

❧

Decisions, decisions!

Michael came home one day and announced to Julia that he had been offered a job in Seattle. It seemed to Julia that he had already made up his mind. "It's a good opportunity, and I think we should go."

Julia was hesitant. She was just beginning to feel at home in western Maryland. She had made some great friends in the neighborhood and had committed herself to working with the youth group at their church. Their children, 12-year-old Jonathan and 10-year-old Misty, were finally happy at school. It seemed to Julia like a bad time to move, even though Michael had been promised a nice increase in salary.

They decided to give it a few days, then talk again, but the thinking didn't help. Michael became more insistent. The more Julia thought about it, the less she liked the idea. It had been difficult enough for the family when they moved to Cumberland four years ago. To traipse all the way across the country again was more than she could handle.

Julia said no.

Michael said yes.

Mutual Influence

Talk together about the ways you get each other to do things. Use sentences like this: "If you want me to do you a favor, then you _____." "One way to get me to do something is to _____."

☙

Jonathan and Misty both said no.

Michael was angered by Julia's attempt to align the children against him and insisted heatedly on yes.

After several days of gridlock, Michael delivered the ultimatum he had hoped to avoid. "I'm going," he said. "You're free to come with me or not. The choice is yours."

Julia sits now at her kitchen table in Seattle and explains her unhappiness to her new friend. "I came because I had to. I didn't want to break up the family, and it appeared that he was willing to do that. That fact haunts me. Now, of course, he claims he wouldn't have left us and wants to convince me of his love and faithfulness. He wants me to forgive him and move on. But how can I? I can't trust that he won't do it again."

She sips her coffee and looks at the understanding face across the table. "That's not the way to make a decision, I know, but it's what we usually do. I've handed him a few ultimatums of my own. Sometimes it seems like the only way we can get ourselves to decide."

Ever faced the decision gridlock that Julia talks about? The battle of wills and ruthless ultimatums that usually follow can tear the trust in your relationship to shreds. How can you proceed when you don't have agreement?

The final style of conversation, heart talk, focuses on that agreement. Your heart is the drive inside you that turns toward the world and seeks in some way to change it. It's been called many things: your will, your spirit, or your intention. Your heart is your soul turned outward. Heart talk, then, expresses your desire to change something.

The nature of that change may shift from moment to moment. You may wish at one moment to save the Brazilian rain forests from destruction and then in a flash want only to get your husband to pick up his dirty socks. While the nature of the desired change may vary, one basic element remains the same: the heart seeks change through encounter.

With most couples, this is a tricky proposition. Trying to instigate change can escalate into a battle of wills. As with Michael and Julia, one says yes, and the other says no. Stubbornness, you will notice, is no stranger to heart talk.

To start, then, it may be helpful to think of these interactions not as attempts to change each other but as attempts to influence each other. Influencing and being influenced are among the joys of marriage. The task of your lifelong relationship is to understand and perfect the wild dynamics in the flow of willpower between you. The point of this chapter is to create a dynamic, decision-making process that works for you and your partner.

PURPOSES OF HEART TALK

When you speak from the heart, you have one of three results in mind. You want your partner to do something, you want your partner to feel something, or you want to control or manipulate your partner. The third choice is obviously not recommended in a loving marriage.

DO SOMETHING

In the first case, heart talk means trying to direct, advise, or persuade your partner along a certain course of behavior. You want something to happen. You want action. At times, statements to this effect may center on simple tasks or errands: "Honey, could you pick up the kids at the day care after work today?" At other times, these statements may tackle much more difficult and complex matters: "I don't want you ever to talk in that tone of voice to my son."

In either case, or in the countless actions and issues you wrestle with in life, the key to heart talk is in expressing yourself in a way that seeks to alter, or at least influence, the actions of your partner. The style of your statements, your tone of voice,

You Are So Beautiful

Remember the song "You Are So Beautiful to Me"? The title expresses the desire to make someone feel loved. Pick five songs that express the way you feel. Burn them onto a CD, and some night soon surprise your partner with your gift.

Good: Play the CD for your partner.

Better: Play the CD, and hum the tunes.

Best: Play the CD, and sing along with gusto!

your level of eye contact, the directness of your speech—all must be gauged to determine which are most likely to be successful.

Ask someone the question "How do you get your partner to do what you want done?" The response is often amusing and always very revealing. Sometimes you'll see a little smile play around the corners of her mouth as your friend thinks through the strategy she uses. Her husband, on the other hand, will stare at you with the completely blank look of a cow before an open gate. He has no idea of what in the world you're talking about. He might even admit it. "I have no clue how to do that. She does exactly what she wants to do when she wants to do it."

Getting your partner to do as you wish usually takes some practice, insight, and skill-building. Many never feel particularly good at it. Michael and Julia both use the same strategy. They play chicken with each other by tossing out escalating ultimatums until one of them finally gives in. Their relationship pays a high price for this gamesmanship. But when done well, mutual influence can be a tremendously rewarding part of your relationship.

FEEL SOMETHING

At other times, heart talk means trying to get your partner to feel something. For the most part, you want the feelings in your marriage to be warm, satisfying, and positive. You want the person you love to feel good most of the time. In so doing, you're not necessarily trying to avoid life's challenges, irritations, or grief but rather attempting to build life on the solid foundation of acceptance and affirmation. In order for this positive feeling to pervade life, couples must constantly touch each other with unconditional expressions of praise, acceptance, and love. These powerful messages surge through the body, soul, mind, and spirit to give life and energy to all the day's activities.

Alternate Days of Adoration

On Monday, Wednesday, and Friday of this week, go to extreme measures to make your partner feel adored. On Tuesday, Thursday, and Saturday, your partner can try to return the favor.

"You're wonderful."

"You're such a hard worker."

"I really respect your loyalty to the people you care about."

If praise sometimes borders on adoration, then so be it. Everyone in this world has a right to be flat-out adored by someone. You're your partner's adoring someone, so don't skimp. Send those messages of praise and love continually and strongly. Work hard to create and sustain that positive feeling.

There are other times in your life together when appropriate feelings are not warm and fuzzy. Feelings of responsibility, sorrow, regret, and remorse can be signs of health. Being in love means you need to see your spouse express the entire spectrum of emotions. Heart talk may involve calling out these intense and difficult feelings. It's delicate work but certainly within the pale of healthy couple heart talk.

Michael's costly ultimatum to Julia hurt her deeply. She's not going to allow Michael to gloss over that pain with a remorseless confession and a demand to move on. She wants him to feel it—not to punish him necessarily but to know that he understands what he did to her. She said it several times before he got it: "I'm really hurt by what you did, and I can't move on until I know that you're truly sorry." This sentence demonstrates a non-controlling, discreet way to provide an opportunity for feeling and expressing regret.

CONTROL

This brings us to the third kind of heart talk. As you've read the descriptions of heart talk and imagined the conversations that might have occurred in your relationship, you may have remembered certain conversations that started out well but went sour. What began as a heart-to-heart discussion disintegrated into a battle for control. Rather than joining in strength, you found yourselves struggling for power. This style of communication may define the way in which personal power is brokered in your relationship. That's why mastering this type of conversation is so important.

Just as heart talk can be used for healthy, affirming purposes, it can also be used negatively. The ability to influence can become power to control. The readiness to affirm can become power to insult. The line between collaborative strength, when members of the couple empower each other to work together, and controlling power, when one person unilaterally controls the other, must never be crossed. Manipulation, control, and insults have no place in a healthy relationship. If these appear, you must take immediate and strong action to address them.

Your communication practices may include, to a greater or lesser extent, words that cut and tear, that hurt and insult. Even if said in half-jest, these patterns will distort both your soul and your relationship. It usually works best to talk about them at a neutral time, when neither of you is upset or angry. Decide what steps you need to take together to eliminate hurtful talk. One way to resolve it is to stop talking the moment it occurs. Remember—no one should be subject to such language involuntarily.

If fighting and insults persist in spite of your best efforts, you may need to consult a professional counselor. Don't accept this kind of talking to each other as normal. There are people who can help you build each other up and not tear each other down.

FRAMEWORKS FOR DECISION

There is genuineness, a certain depth we recognize when we use the expression "speaking from the heart." The words require us to sit up and take notice. If you hear your partner say, "Honey, we need to have a heart-to-heart talk," you know that the request is for a conversation of importance and significance. You may sometimes hear these words and get a squeamish feeling in

What Not to Say—Ever!

All couples need a pact for mutual respect. Each of you draw up a list of words, phrases, and tones that feel disrespectful. Form an agreement to apologize immediately if they appear and to gradually eliminate these words or phrases from your conversations.

the pit of your stomach, because you know the conversation may be not only deep and penetrating but also difficult.

How do these heart-to-heart talks work? What are the patterns that drive them? And how can you use these patterns to create good decisions?

The first step involves charting a clear decision-making framework. The following seven-step method can be modified to suit the unique dynamics and characteristics of your relationship. It will probably work fairly well for many of the problems you're trying to solve.

1. Clearly identify the problem.
2. Brainstorm together for possible solutions. This requires that you both place on the table a number of possible solutions or directions without stopping to critique or evaluate them.
3. Soul-search using the same outline as in brainstorming, but quickly enumerate matters of the soul (emotions, dreams, memories, and myths) that pertain to this problem.
4. From the list of possibilities you've just compiled, begin whittling them down until you're left with just two or three.
5. From the two or three, choose the one you both seem most comfortable with.
6. Set a course of action, detailing the responsibilities each of you has in carrying out your choice.
7. Set an exact time in the future when you can sit down again together and evaluate what you've done.

Given the discussion of various forms of intelligence in chapter three, you've probably guessed by now that this seven-step process has a weakness. It works best when both members of the problem-solving team think alike in most respects. For example, if together you're strong in the logical-mathematical intelligence, or if both of you possess similar linguistic gifts, these seven steps will likely have led you to an agreement. Such agreements create clear, strong decisions and a true sense of teamwork.

But what happens if you approach the issue so differently that reaching a blended and compromised agreement proves to be beyond your ability? When agreement appears impossible, you may find yourselves agreeing to disagree. This can be done cheerfully and enthusiastically once the negative stigma of disagreement has been abolished. In fact, disagreement can be a sign of health in a relationship.

With some problems and issues, agreeing to disagree brings you to the end of the conversation. For example, you can agree to disagree about whether you support a particular politician, judge a certain movie as worth seeing, or find poetry stimulating. These conversations and decisions can all be hashed over interminably or left completely alone as you please. But other situations may not offer the luxury of inertia. A teenage daughter consistently ignoring her curfew, aging parents approaching the limits of their ability to live independently, or spending habits that jeopardize your security are problems that require action whether you reach agreement or not.

In such cases, healthy couples usually end up choosing one member's perspective over the other. For example, say you're strong in the logical-mathematical intelligence, and your partner excels in the outward personal intelligences, numbers 3 and 7 respectively in Gardiner's scheme. You'll probably disagree strongly regarding how to deal with your teenage daughter's curfew violations. In the end, you may decide that your partner's gifts may hold more promise of a successful outcome. You agree to disagree about how you may approach it, but you choose which one of your gifts will actually be used in dealing with the situation.

The following six-step process suggests that agreeing to disagree does not necessarily lead to gridlock.

1. Identify the problem clearly.
2. Brainstorm as in the seven-step process.
3. Soul-search as in the seven-step process.
4. Seeing no chance of bringing these ideas and perspectives into a blended, compromised solution, choose which one of you will handle the problem.
5. Identify the ways in which the second partner can support the first and reinforce the solution as it unfolds.
6. Identify an exact time in the future when you can sit together and evaluate.

If you're the partner stepping back, be sure that your support is strong and steady. Give the other way a fair chance to work. If you're the partner stepping forward, be sure to keep the communication lines open with your spouse. Even if one of you takes the lead, you both still deeply need each other.

With these frameworks in place, the conversational guidelines in the next chapter will help establish healthy heart talk in your relationship.

fourteen

THE APPLE OF DECISION

∿

The bright autumn sun sparkles on the deep redness of apples so abundant and large that the branches bend and strain to hold them. Inside each red orb lies the seeds that will carry forward the characteristics of that tree. The apple tree's history and the future are locked inside those essence-bearing seeds. The crisp, pungent air smells of fullness, wholeness, and completion.

Heart talk acts like an apple seed. It carries the essence of your soul outward into the world, seeking fulfillment. When you speak from the heart, you try to express the deepest desires and longings in such a way that things on the outside change. In this way, heart talk and soul talk differ. Soul talk seeks understanding and affirmation. Heart talk wants action. Soul talk leads to deep knowledge. Heart talk pushes for change.

It takes courage, strength, determination, and perseverance to change anything in the world. You must be strong. Only a person with a brave heart will get results. The weak-of-heart give up quickly and thus never see their desires fulfilled, their goals met, or their feelings responded to. But remember—just getting your way is not the purpose of heart talk. Taking the steps to get what you need involves a complex dialogue with your partner.

Heart talk involves your partner's wishes as well as your own. You need to speak in such a way that the decision you make together reckons with all combined perspectives. Talking and listening in heart talk use the acronyms HEART and AP-PLE.

TALKING

When talking, speak from your HEART: give your partner a heads-up, use emotion and reason, and then translate your thoughts into a direct request for action.

HEADS UP

As in all conversation, the speaker can help smooth the process with a clear indication of intent. As you start the conversation, designate clearly that you want to talk heart-to-heart. Persuasion brings complexities and challenges to a conversation that are not found in the other conversational styles. Heart talk aims to change the actions or feelings of your partner. Surprise attacks are not advisable here. They almost always backfire. Give your partner plenty of warning by offering a "heads-up" about your intention.

This heads-up does not need to be complicated. A few words will suffice to make the direction and intention of the conversation clear to your partner.

"Honey, there's something I want you to do."

"Something you've been doing lately is bothering me. Is now a good time to talk about it?"

"Could we talk heart-to-heart?"

"Sweetie, about those dirty socks . . ."

EMOTION

Your heart is your soul turned outward. Your soul, therefore, plays a vital part in determining what you want to have happen in your relationship. You need to communicate your soul's burden. It will motivate your partner.

The process of making a decision never calls upon reason alone but needs a good mixture of the soul as well. As you and your partner face a decision, you'll want to express your feelings about possibilities. You'll want to examine how any direction you take affects the hopes and dreams you've held onto for years. Bringing all the aspects of soul to bear on a decision provides you with a wealth of considerations that can only enrich your choices. Heart talk usually incorporates a good shot of soul talk along the way.

This is the first of two complicating loops in heart talk. To make a good decision, you must express what you feel about your choices. As we said in section four, expressing your feelings calls for soul talk. It's important to recognize and signal to your partner whenever you make the transition to soul talk so adjustments in the listening posture can be made. Remember that soul talk requires that the listener suspend judgment or contradiction but affirm the talker. In heart talk, however, questioning, evaluating, and contradicting comprise the very substance of the conversation.

Here lies an apparent contradiction. It happens whenever the soul loop enters the heart talk process. Failure to recognize and understand this apparent contradiction is the downfall of countless couple conversations and the root of many couples' inability to make decisions together. Here's the way to handle this loop.

When one of you is speaking from the soul (emotion, imagination, memory, and myth) while in the decision-making or change-making mode, both of you must go out through this loop together. That is, you must skip back to the guidelines for soul talk and engage as talker and listener, using the acronyms you mastered in section four: SOUL and LEAF.

This can be confusing, but hold on. The soul loop is vitally important to good decisions. Let the entire loop run its natural course right there in the middle of heart talk. When completed, and the F of LEAF indicates that you are both satisfied, then return again to your heart talk, knowing deeply what your partner feels about the choices in your decision.

Be on the lookout for two dangers in the soul loop. The first of these dangers, soul loop omission, arises when the loop is not given its due. Either the one who has strong feelings squelches them and omits them from the conversation, or the listener fails to follow the LEAF format and prevents those feelings from being fully heard. In either case, strong feelings are left out of the conversation and will therefore have no bearing on the decision you make. The decision is thus doomed to failure. You'll never be truly committed to a decision that does not involve your passion. Weak conversations lead to weak decisions.

For Dominic and Natalie, soul loop omission created a series of questionable decisions about Aimee's curfew. Dominic was not comfortable with Natalie's feelings about her daughter's development and would cut off her expression of them. He believed that bringing in feelings at the point of decision would only cloud his clear thinking. Natalie grew tired of fighting about it and would relent. Dominic's laying down the law on Aimee proved to be ill-advised, partly because it was soulless. Natalie's emotion was a necessary part of this decision, and once that was settled, things with Aimee became much more manageable.

The second danger is soul loop runaway. It's the opposite of omission. Rather than being left out, the strong feelings of one come to dominate the conversation and predetermine the outcome of the conversation. In this case, you may follow the soul talk loop, but you stay out there, continually looping the circle and never coming home to the business of heart talk. Soul loop runaway assumes that the expression of strong feelings is all there is to decision-making. This steals the opportunity of your partner to evaluate what you have said.

Many things can cause soul loop runaway. Tears can stop the conversation dead in its tracks. A raised voice can end the conversation out there in the soul talk loop and tip the decision in the favor of the one who yells. When the soul loop enters the conversation, it tries to bring the deeper elements of each of you into the process. These elements need to influence the decision but never control it. You must never take away from your partner the right and responsibility to evaluate the impact your feelings should have on the decision you're making together.

Your partner may appreciate and affirm your feelings yet still remain unconvinced that they necessitate the change of direction you're asking for. When feelings are used to dictate rather than motivate behavior in your spouse, then you've crossed the line into manipulation.

Motivate your spouse to change as best you can by expressing your feelings and dreams and all aspects of your soul. Express them as you learned to in section four. But remember that your partner will evaluate what you're sharing, and the two of you will incorporate those considerations into your decision in a way that fits for both of you.

REASON

If you want to influence your partner's action, you'll generally need to have some good reasons. Providing good reasons, as explained in chapter three, involves mind talk. But there's a significant difference when mind talk appears to simply talk something through, solve a problem, or enjoy a discussion, as in that chapter, and when it appears with the intent to persuade your partner to do or feel something. This mind talk is a horse of a different color. You're asking for action, and that action must be voluntarily embraced. Your listener has the right and the obligation to evaluate your request and to question the validity of your reasons for asking.

Affirmation or Evaluation

Pick an emotion such as sadness, anger, fear, love, or frustration. Identify five times when you've expressed that emotion and sought affirmation from your partner, as in soul talk. Then identify five other times when you needed that emotion to be evaluated, as in heart talk.

Is it always clear to your partner which you seek?

When you offer good reasons to move a decision in a certain direction, you enter the second loop of heart talk—the mind loop. The mind loop acts much like the soul loop as it uses your skills in mind talk. The same dangers appear. Mind loop omission happens when you don't bring reason into the decision-making conversation. Mind loop runaway occurs when the whole process is shut down based solely on the logic of one person.

With this in mind, you'll need to express your reasons clearly and boldly, but don't assume that simple reasoning will create the change in your partner that you're looking for. Speak strongly, but also invite your spouse to be equally thorough and bold in placing your reasons under the microscope of analysis. Expect resistance and embrace refusal as ways of hammering out a direction that will suit both of you. Heart talk is not for the weak or wimpy.

TRANSLATE

The final step in heart talk is to state clearly what it is that you want from your partner. This response is the key to this style, but many times couples leave this step undone. If you want your thoughts and emotions to translate into some specific action or response from your partner, then say it in a way that leaves no room for misunderstanding.

"I'm asking you to forgive me."

"I want you to stop touching me that way in public."

"I want you to keep to the budget we both agreed to."

Good, old-fashioned negotiating may follow. The clear expression of your wishes doesn't obligate your partner—it simply gives you both a place to start. At times your negotiations will be as sweet as cherry chocolates. At other times they'll test your ability to stay focused, connected, and caring. But unless your partner knows what you want, a true and measured response can't take shape.

LISTENING

The listening side of heart talk will challenge you. Your partner is trying to get you to do something you may or may not feel like doing. The greatest danger in listening to heart talk, then, is to lose yourself. That is, to give up what's truly you in order satisfy your partner. Giving yourself up in this case presents itself as an inauthentic process that may yield a temporary peace or an ephemeral agreement, only to end after time in disappointment, conflict, or depression.

What is needed to find this authenticity? How can you listen to the driving force and desires of your partner and not be swept away like a palm tree in a hurricane? Your ability to maintain the stability and strength to stand your ground while also listening well may be helped by remembering the APPLE: anticipate, pause, pull together, listen, and evaluate.

ANTICIPATE

The balance of any relationship reveals itself in the context of heart talk. This is the dimension of push and pull, of negotiation, of power struggles, and of intention. These conversations are therefore among your most complex and difficult. Anticipation of the difficulties before you enter on the listening side of heart talk can help you a great deal.

The most important thing to keep in mind as you prepare to listen in a heart-to-heart conversation is that you're being invited into action. Sometimes it may feel more as if you're being pushed. In either case, your partner wants you to do or feel something, and you will be required to make a choice about that request. Heart talk demands that you be both open and centered—a combination sometimes difficult to attain. Make sure you know what your listening role is here, and anticipate that this conversation may not be a sunny walk in the park but rather a sterner test of your strength and resolve.

Anticipate not only difficulty but also success. If you and your partner commit to finding equitable and mutually satisfying conclusions to these conversations, then you'll make it happen. Positive anticipation will help you continue to work, continue to try, and continue to push for a resolution. You can both get what you want and what you need from each other through heart talk.

PAUSE

Heart talk eschews hurry. You're being asked to do something, and whether that something is great or small, pressure to rush to your decision will distort your judgment. A pause to slow things down nearly always moves you closer to a decision you can live with comfortably. That's why the sales pitch you hear on television urges you to call now. The reduced time empowers the message.

Your pauses may need to last a few moments or a few days. The nature of the situation and your partner's request will help determine that. The important factor in the pause of listening is to empower you, the listener, to feel comfortable with the process and therefore more comfortable with your response.

PULL YOURSELF TOGETHER

Listening in heart talk requires that you listen to two voices at the same time. Your partner's voice expresses the desires and needs you're being asked to respond to. You also must listen to your own inner voice, the voice of your soul, to help determine what your responses might be and what choices you'll deem it possible to make. Your ability to calmly stay in touch with this deep, inner part of yourself means being centered.

When you start to feel pressured by your partner's words, or if a request begins to turn into a demand, then the push to move you off center increases. In these cases, use the strategies you've developed to stay within yourself.

Close your eyes and breathe deeply.

Touch a certain icon or piece of jewelry that steadies you.

Assume a calm and restful posture, or move your body in a way that heightens restfulness and peace.

Heart-to-heart conversations can become escalating power struggles. If this happens and all else fails, take a time out to regain your center.

LISTEN

Anyone who attempts to persuade you to choose a course of action has two forms of argument: the rational and the emotional. When you turn on your television set, you find yourself bombarded with both forms of persuasion as advertisers try to get you to buy their products. Your parents, your children, and your partner have also mastered these persuasive techniques. As they speak, you'll need to stop and consider what they're asking you to do.

As you've seen, in heart talk your partner is attempting to get you to do something or to feel something. These attempts take the form of persuasive arguments that center alternatively on the rational or on the emotional. Your partner will be talking to you from the mind or from the soul. Listening, therefore, gets complicated. As listener, you must identify the dimension your partner is speaking from and then apply your listening skills that coincide with that dimension.

If your partner speaks from the mind, you'll follow your listening skills explained in the acronym BRANCH. If the argument takes on a more imaginative or emotional tone, you'll apply the skills explained in the acronym LEAF. These skills were mastered in earlier chapters. This switching can be difficult at first, but with practice you can make these transitions seamlessly.

Be sure to take time to follow the listening process thoroughly. Sometimes the pressure of a decision causes a listener to rush through this process, and vital elements of the discussion are omitted. It will be very difficult, for example, for your partner to trust your resistance to an idea if not convinced that you have first attended carefully to the reasons offered to support that idea.

EVALUATE

The final step in heart talk listening is to evaluate what you've heard. In evaluation you decide whether the attempts and urgings of your spouse are sufficiently strong to move you into action. How compelling are your partner's reasons? What emotions are involved, and how much influence should they have in making your choice about what to do? Is there a compromise that you could propose? How much can you give without compromising yourself? How should the broader contextual elements such as family, community, and faith play into this process?

These questions swirl through the mind of the active listener as you talk heart to heart with your partner. They are part and parcel of the process of evaluation and will help protect you from doing things you don't really want to do.

At the end of the talking process in heart talk, your partner asks you to enter the rough-and-tumble experience of negotiation and the decision frameworks discussed earlier. You can begin to negotiate, however, only when you have determined your own wishes, intentions, and ideas. Standing on that solid ground, you may enter the negotiations with confidence. You'll know where you can bend and where you can't. You'll be assured that as you and your partner move toward consensus, the outcome will contain that which is deeply important to both of you.

The key to successfully talking heart to heart lies not in doing it perfectly but in being persistent. It's important for both partners to vigorously protect the turbulent and sometimes zany process of logical and emotional evaluation.

fifteen

MARRIAGE NATION

ॐ

Think of your marriage as a nation. The similarities will appear quickly in your mind. First, both usually have a few important founding documents that spell out the reasons they exist and set forth their basic structure. In the United States, the Declaration of Independence, the Bill of Rights, and the Constitution fulfill this role. Other nations have different but equally important documents. Your marriage began with marriage vows, a marriage license, and perhaps a few love letters to spice things up. These documents tell the tale of the profound commitment you made to each other—your marriage covenant.

Second, your country and your marriage both thrive in the middle of a dizzy array of systems and forces. Your country struggles with worldwide movements in economics, power, and politics. The broader family of nations exerts pressure, support, and conflict in varying amounts. In the same way, your marriage works in constant touch with other couples, your extended families, and various interested parties such as work, government, and faith community. Sometimes these contacts prove helpful and supportive, sometimes not. The concentric circles of influence that surround you all participate in the context of your marriage.

Destiny marks the third similarity. Your country believes it has a purpose for existing. That purpose holds together its people and directs the kinds of decisions they make. When this sense of purpose dries up, the nation is sure to die. Your marriage also has a sense of purpose. You and your partner were brought together by God to fulfill a higher purpose than either of your could attain alone. This higher purpose, this destiny, is your calling.

Covenant, context, and calling: when it comes time to make a decision, each of these three components has its contribution to make. While these influences may not always be comfortable or positive, and you may even be quarreling with one or more of them, your best decisions will consider their input.

In this chapter, three couples will illustrate the way these pathways work to bring clarity, integrity, and sometimes complications to decisions. Good choices require guidance, whether you're deciding to recycle your grocery bags, buy a new car, restructure the way the housework gets done, or have a child. The following three pathways do not spell out an exhaustive list, but they show the basic shape of the wonderful world you live in. As you contemplate and use these pathways, your decision will better reflect your values and the interests.

PATHWAY 1: COVENANT

Start with your marriage vows. You may have used a traditional religious ceremony or a modern version, or you may have written your vows. In any case, bring them out again for another look. These vows expressed your dreams and desires for your marriage. They mention the permanence and faithfulness of your relationship. While they may not include everything you felt in your heart on your wedding day, they express the essence of the commitment you made. The agreement that you have as a couple constitutes a guide for your heart. What are the basic principles and commitments the two of you have to each other and to the relationship?

Remember Natalie and Dominic from chapter seven? They're struggling with Aimee, Natalie's teenage daughter. Their issue of raising Aimee together came up early in their relationship. Natalie made it clear that nothing serious would happen without a commitment to her daughter. She always said it with a smile, but her words carried a sting: "Love me—love my daughter. We come as a package deal." Dominic didn't bat an eye, and Natalie knew she had found a man she could trust.

It was this strength in Dominic that Natalie loved right from the start of their relationship. Part of her expectations in their marriage involved his partnering role in raising Aimee, especially when she hit those teenage years. Natalie remembered the hell she had put her own mother through and had no reason to think that Aimee would be any different when her turn came along. While there are some problems in reaching agreements about how to handle Aimee, these two are committed to doing the best job they can. They agree that it's part of being married. It wasn't stated in their marriage ceremony, but both agree that it's part of their covenant with each other.

What's in your covenant? While your covenant is unique to you, some key ideas usually find their way into most relationships.

Many couples believe that there's a basic understanding of equality between the two partners. One is not going to lord it over the other or make decisions without the other's input. Mutual respect grows under a clear sense of equality.

Balance also comes into the picture. With the pressures of today's fast-paced and demanding life, the sense of sharing responsibilities and tasks keeps the practical stresses of living from falling on just one pair of shoulders. Though specific responsibilities may differ, each spouse generally wants to know that the other is also pulling his or her fair share of the load.

Another guiding principle in your relationship may be the desire for the empowerment of each partner. You may seek to help each other become stronger and more confident as individuals. You recognize that a strong, healthy marriage grows from the strength and health in each person. You want to encourage and support each other to pursue and achieve goals and interests.

Concerns such as equality, balance, and empowerment form a substantial part of your relational covenant. You may also have other principles that you've included. Clarity about all aspects of your covenant will help you in joint decision-making.

PATHWAY 2: CONTEXT

No marriage is an island. Voices, expectations, intentions, and legacies from outside surround you and your partner and contribute in their own ways to your decision. These contributors take many forms and faces, including family, your community, the company you work for, or the ideas and principles that you believe in. Being open and interactive with these surrounding forces can be especially helpful when you're trying to reach the decisions that are involved in heart talk. They can also make life very complicated.

Caesar and Leola had been married 22 years and were busy launching the oldest of their four children when Caesar's family issues bulldozed into their life. Caesar's family followed a stern, conservative Christian viewpoint. His father ran the house with a steel will and an iron hand. He saw the world locked in a struggle of good and evil—there was no middle ground. "My father's decisions were never questioned."

Unfortunately, the practice of splitting everything into either good or evil filtered down to the way he saw his two sons, Caesar and Tomas. Caesar filled the role of the good son, and Tomas took the role of the bad. Many such families ostracize the "bad" brother, sending him out without support, to get what he "deserves." But this family was different. Tomas was kept within the family circle and taken care of. He became a mission of mercy to his parents, and they inadvertently created a son dependent on their largess. As he grew older and established his independence, Caesar was expected to join them in caring for his unfortunate brother.

When his parents died, Caesar felt obligated to continue this care. But his brother, now 43 years old, lived 2,000 miles away, suffered bad health, and was unable and unwilling to do anything for himself. True to his deceased father's wishes, Caesar stepped up to help. He moved Tomas to an apartment close to him and promised to provide for him.

Leola didn't resist the move, but decisions from then on were filled with angst and conflict between them. Supporting Tomas proved to be a drain on the family's finances that they were barely able to handle. Holiday celebrations usually included an invitation to Tomas to join them, but he constantly complained about the traditions and rituals they followed. Even meals became a problem. One day Tomas announced he would not return if his brother continued to use a certain table prayer of thanksgiving he found offensive. Caesar promised not to use it again. Leola hit the roof.

She was tempted to insist that Tomas grow up and get a life of his own, but Leola knew such a break would swamp Caesar with guilt. He would see it as a betrayal of his family, a swipe at his deceased parents, and an abandonment of his responsibilities as the good son. Leola tried to understand this while simultaneously working to prevent the toll of Caesar's overachieving habits from overwhelming their marriage and family. Financially and relationally, they were approaching bottom.

No easy button exists for Caesar and Leola. They face a daunting task: find a way to deal with Tomas that respects but is not bound by Caesar's family legacy while also remaining true to themselves, their relationship, and their children. The task is a difficult one, and the solution is very complex. Hope rests for them in their willingness to work together to use the strength of the family and the loyalty of Caesar to bring about a mutually acceptable course of action.

Your context, like that of Caesar and Leola, fills your marriage with similar strengths and challenges. What are some of the ways your families have enriched your lives? What are some of the problems you've had bringing your family legacies into your marriage?

Similar questions arise as you move through the concentric circles of influence in your life. Your community, your faith tradition, and the company you work for all have certain expectations of you and your partner. Each has its own "will" that may alter the decisions you make. As you make decisions together, be sure to consider the contributions of these forces.

PATHWAY 3: CALLING

Is there inspiration and direction for marriage that come from a higher source than context? Many couples desire to place their religious faith or spiritual beliefs at the center of their relationship. This allows the strength of faith to bring your relationship under the influence of strong traditions of wisdom and love. It also may bring along beliefs and practices that offer further guidelines or expectations for your relationship.

Your faith may have much to say about the purpose of your relationship. Couples are often gifted with the conviction that they have a high purpose to fulfill. You may have said it yourself: "We believe that we were brought together for a purpose." Just how you were brought together may sometimes seem to others to be coincidental. But for you, purpose has guided every step. The conviction of purpose shines as clear as crystal.

Purpose goes by many names: "the will of God," "divine intent," or simply "Providence." Your personal beliefs will guide the name you choose, but all are informed by the sense that a magnificent purpose above and beyond us guides and directs our lives. It is our task to conform our intentions and our lives to this greater purpose. Emerson refers to this task when he says that the education of our will is the object of our lives. It is what Paul means when he urges his readers to stop conforming to the patterns of the world around them but to be transformed by the mind's renewal. "Then," he says, "you will be able to test and approve what God's will is" (Rom. 12:2). Paul goes on to describe that will as "good, pleasing, and perfect."

What are you living for? That question surprised Alex and Christine.

Christine accepted Alex's proposal for marriage with grace and enthusiasm, attributing his dry throat and the slight catch in his words to nervousness. After all, he had never asked anyone to marry him before. She appreciated the elaborate plans he had made in asking some of their friends to play soft, romantic music among the trees while the moon rose over the lake and he bent down on one knee.

As word spread about their engagement, Alex and Christine were greeted with joy and encouragement. They were a popular couple with many friends and supporters. Alex was just finishing his final year of seminary training, and Christine's job as a social worker at the hospital was both challenging and satisfying. Everyone agreed they were the perfect couple.

Well, almost everyone. Christine's mother, Joyce, was not excited about her daughter's engagement. While she respected Christine's independence and choice, she had some questions for her.

"Christine, this home we've always lived in is not a mansion for sure, but it's very nice, and we know you're aware of the privilege you enjoyed growing up in this place and in this neighborhood. I know you love Alex, but can you be happy with him? A home like this, the camp on the lake, the vacations we've taken, these things are not going to be possible on a minister's salary.

On another day a different concern was raised. "Christine, the other day I saw an article that said that ministers move every three years on average. I can see that you love him, but is that really healthful? And when you have children, won't moving so often affect them negatively?"

And Christine's mother was not totally convinced Alex's theology was right. "Christine, you know how important our beliefs and our church are to your father and me. And we've tried to pass that on to you. We love the fact that Alex wants to be a pastor, but frankly, we're concerned about his beliefs. Aren't you going to have trouble with some of his liberal ideas?"

These questions were difficult for Christine to answer, not because she was also concerned about material things or Alex's theology. But the pain she heard in her mother's voice caught her off guard. She realized that beneath this round of questions, her mother was hitting a significant and as yet unresolved issue between Alex and her. She later surprised Alex with a question of her own.

"Is love enough to marry for?"

"Wh-what?" She recognized the catch in his voice. She had heard it before.

"Shouldn't marriage be aimed at something bigger than love?" She was a bit surprised at the way the question came out, but she let it stand.

Alex was about to spout the many things he envisioned doing with Christine by his side, but her uneasiness stopped him short. This was more than another of their intellectual discussions about marriage. He turned and faced her.

"Say more."

The discussion that followed spun Alex and Christine into weeks of challenge and soul-searching. Convinced of their love, they were determined to discover how their union fit into the grand scheme of God and the world around them. The questions they asked themselves may be questions for you and your spouse to wrestle with also.

"Why have we been brought together?"

"What do we have to contribute?"

"How can we enter the flow of God's will?"

"At this stage in life, what are the purposes of our marriage?"

Only as answers to these questions began to clarify could Christine return to her mother and answer her questions with strength.

Any couple who seeks answers to these questions will develop a uniting theme that can inspire their lives daily. For many, a large part of this purpose has to do with raising a family. Having and guiding children is truly a high calling and responsibility. Another couple may be united in their efforts to continue the family business, to work for peace among the races, or to produce beauty in our world. Whatever your purpose may be, see it as a gift from above, and work diligently for it. Living your marriage with purpose is the way soul runs through you and enters the world.

A clear sense of call can influence every decision you make. You're continuously asking, "How does this particular choice fit into my higher purpose?" Couples who can successfully integrate their own individual intentions, the guidelines of their relational covenant, and the calling of their higher purpose are sure to accomplish something wonderful in this world. If that sounds a bit overwhelming, don't worry. The complexity of this integration keeps most of us from feeling as though we've ever got it completely right. But that's okay. Just keep working on it, struggling with it, and celebrating the times when things begin to fall into place.